Vegetarian Cats & Dogs

Vegetarian Cats & Dogs

James A. Peden

Harbingers of a New Age
Troy Montana
1992

To the memory of Little Tyke,
for her love and inspiration

This book is not meant to replace your veterinarian. Neither the author nor publisher can be held responsible for any adverse reactions to recommendations contained in this book. Seek a veterinarian (preferably holistic) for specific conditions that might warrant expert treatment.

Address correspondence to:
Harbingers of a New Age
717 E. Missoula Avenue
Troy MT 59935

Copyright © 1992 by Harbingers of A New Age
Library of Congress Catalog Card Number 90-082536
ISBN 0-941319-01-6

Foreword

I enjoyed reading the first edition of *Dogs & Cats Go Vegetarian* for many reasons. I enjoyed the philosophical and spiritual concepts that were balanced by the lengthy and finally successful search for scientifically based vegetarian recipes for both dogs and cats.

I have recommended this book to many of my clients and they have been pleased with its contents and with the practical and relatively easy ways to provide delicious and nutritious diets for their pets.

In my opinion, the most important part of the new edition is the chapter called "They Are Doing It." The many successful and enthusiastic experiences of those changing their pet's diet from a commercial to a vegetarian fare should inspire many more to follow their lead. As a veterinarian being concerned with the animal's health, it is very encouraging to observe health improving in many cases after being on the new regimen.

I feel that this book will continue to play a vital part in the ongoing transformation of our present culture to a more loving, caring one tht will place a much higher value on both human and animal life. As we observe the gentle, loving influence upon the lion — Little Tyke, and the many dogs and cats responding dramatically to this influence, perhaps we can view this as a microcosm and then visualize the larger macrocosm of a gentle humankind where they are neither involved in the slaughtering of other humans nor of animals. We can then see this powerful force, influencing the animals to adjust their behaviors to be more in harmony with the peaceful Biblical prophecy concerning the calf lying down with the lion.

Michael W. Lemmon, DVM

————————

Michael Lemmon, a veterinarian based in Renton, Washington, practices both holistic and allopathic medicine in his practice at the Highlands Veterinary Hospital. He has spent a lifetime exploring the natural healing methods resulting from his study of iridology, herbology, and massage. His specialties are classical homeopathy, acupuncture and nutrition.

He serves on the boards of the American Holistic Veterinary Medical Association, and well as the Resort of the Mountains, a rustic retreat center specializing in health care, cleansing and rejuvenation.

Preface

I CAN STILL REMEMBER, AS A BOY, THE REJOICINGS
OVER THE CLOSING OF THE LAST SLAUGHTERHOUSE.
H. G. WELLS: *A Modern Utopia*

Along the Rogue River in southern Oregon, my wife and I opened a book and organic food store in 1974. It featured a selection of books focusing on a world without sickness and war.

The store was more for our research than for the few people who shopped there. We couldn't have survived on just the store's earnings. Fortunately, in the back part of the building a crew produced *Sun Bars*.

I began manufacturing these fruit and nut bars in 1972, selling them nationwide through health and natural food stores. To us they were vehicles for messages that burned our souls. We printed "sayings" on the *Sun Bar* label backs and customers loved them, writing how just the right words came at the right time. With scores available at any one time, we published hundreds in the course of four million *Sun Bars*. They subsidized the store, and we pored over book catalogs.

Devouring books on birth and physiological growth, I took time out to deliver our first born. My background in chemistry and math proved a reliable foundation.

Years passed, and we went to mail order. By this time the family included three children, cats and a dog. Wanting something more for the catalog, I thought of writing about vegetarian pets.

As my wife slept one night, I wrote a 20-page treatise and called it *Dogs & Cats Go Vegetarian*. It began with the futuristic quote by Wells that garnered my feelings so well. In *A Modern Utopia* he writes:

> In all the round world of Utopia; there is no meat. There used to be. But now we cannot stand the thought of slaughterhouses. In a population that is all educated, and at about the same level of physical refinement, it is practically impossible to find anyone who will hew a dead ox or pig.

Rereading that first manuscript, little then did I realize the magnitude of this project: formulating a valid way of feeding cats (and dogs) without animal products. It took hundreds of hours of research, from absorbing obscure scientific journals in veterinary schools to engaging scientists scattered around the world. Not the least was feedback from willing participants, some of whose stories are in these chapters.

Obviously a book such as this benefited from many hands. Thanks to Lynn Burns (the former Barbara Lynn Peden) who initially shared my vision. My appreciation goes to the many scientists (some of whom personally shared their thoughts) responsible for uncovering the precise dietary requirements for our animal friends. Thanks to supportive veterinarians who expressed gratitude to us for doing a needed service. Thanks go to the early pioneers, too numerous to name, who validated this research with their own experiences. Thanks to the thousands now using *Vegepet* supplements, supporting Harbingers of a New Age in its ongoing research and development efforts.

Finally, gratitude goes to my wonderful wife, Kathi. Although not present at the beginning, she willingly came aboard and enthusiastically caught the dream.

Contents

APPENDICES

CHARTS

Chapter 1

LION LIGHTS

At four years old the mature African lioness weighed 352 pounds. Her body stretched 10 feet 4 inches long and could run 40 miles per hour. Her skull, highly adapted to killing and eating prey, possessed short, powerful jaws. Normally, African lions eat gnus, zebras, gazelles, impalas, and giraffes. This particular big cat, in her prime and perfect health, chose a more gentle way of life, vegetarian!

A violent birth

Georges and Margaret Westbeau, standing outside the thick steel bars of the cage, watched nervously. Inside, a vicious, raging beast baring razor claws and glistening fangs, roared. Flinging herself at the couple, who watched from barely three feet away, her suffering amber eyes defied their presence.

Always, in the past, this lioness destroyed her offspring as soon as they were born. Four times in the last seven years, her powerful jaws had crushed her newborn cubs, furiously throwing them against her cage's bars where they tumbled, lifeless.

Denying the normal instincts of motherhood, what possessed this lioness? Her life mocked its former freedom. She lived a caged animal, taken from the wild and tortured by those who captured her. Did she feel that by destroying her cubs they would be spared the humiliation that she endured?

Suddenly, the newborn cub came flying towards the people anxiously watching. Georges quickly grabbed the cub through the bars before it could be killed. Its right front leg dangled helplessly from its mother's brutal jaws. In the face of such fury the only thing the human could say was, "You poor little tyke."

The Westbeaus took the three-pound "Little Tyke" to their Hidden Valley Ranch near Seattle and there it joined the menagerie of other animals including horses, cattle, and chickens. Curious peacocks lined the housetop, kittens peered through a picket fence, and two terriers danced with joy for the new addition to the household.

Drinking bottles of warm milk, Little Tyke began the long road to recovery.

Mysterious reaction

With the advice of experts the Westbeaus began weaning Little Tyke onto solid food at three months. Leaving only a favorite doll, they removed most of her rubber toys, replacing them with bones from a freshly slaughtered beef. They carried the small cub to the bones. Unexpectedly, she violently threw up!

Experts told them in no uncertain terms that lions couldn't live without meat. In the wild, lions ate only flesh — eleven pounds a day for an adult female. Alarmed at Little Tyke's strange behavior, they wondered at how they could introduce meat into her diet? In the meantime, they continued feeding Little Tyke baby cereal mixed with milk.

A well meaning friend suggested mixing beef blood with milk, in increasing proportions. Given milk containing ten drops of blood, Little Tyke would have nothing to do with it. They mixed in five drops of blood, and hid that bottle. As she sucked on the plain milk they quickly switched bottles. Again she refused it. In desperation they added *one* drop of blood to a full bottle of milk, but Little Tyke refused this bottle as well, and they could only stare in amazement.

Another friend suggested putting plain milk in one hand, and milk mixed with hamburger in the palm of the other hand. Little Tyke readily licked the milk from one hand, but when Georges changed hands, she immediately turned away. Sensing her distress, Georges wiped his hands on a nearby towel and picked her up. Hissing in fear and cringing away, she looked sick from the danger-smell of meat on his hand. She only settled down when given a fresh bottle of milk held in washed hands.

Thousand-dollar reward

At nine months old and weighing sixty-five pounds, Little Tyke had the splints and bandages on her leg taken off for the last time. She slowly learned to depend on the healed leg, and mingled with other animals on the ranch.

Since the ranch didn't earn enough income to make ends meet, the Westbeaus ran a small cold storage plant in town. Little Tyke came with them when they went to work and word got around about this vegetarian lioness. When she was four years old, the Westbeaus advertised a thousand dollar reward for anyone who could devise a method tricking Little Tyke into eating meat. Numerous plans met with failure since Little Tyke refused to have anything to do with flesh.

The answer

The caretakers of this gentle animal sought out animal experts, always asking them about diet. Finally, one young visitor set their mind at ease. With serious eyes he turned to them and asked, "Don't you read your *Bible?* Read Genesis 1:30, and you will get your answer." At his first opportunity Georges read in astonishment, "And to every beast of the earth, and to every fowl of the air, and to everything that creepeth upon the earth, wherein there is life, I have given every green herb for meat: and it was so." At that point, after four years, the Westbeaus finally stopped worrying.

Little Tyke's meals

A typical meal consisted of various grains, chosen for their protein, calcium, fats, and roughage. Margaret always cooked a few days' supply ahead of time. At feeding time, a double handful of the cooked grains along with one-half gallon of milk with two eggs, supplied Little Tyke a delicious meal. She had one condition before eating. Her favorite rubber doll had to be right next to her!

For teeth and gums, the Westbeaus supplied rubber boots since she refused bones. They attracted her to the boots by sprinkling them with perfume. One boot lasted almost a month.

Little Tyke had many close animal friends. Her favorites were Pinky (a kitten), Imp (another kitten), Becky (a lamb) and Baby (a fawn). Her favorite and closest friend, however, was Becky, who preferred Little Tyke's company to any of the other animals.

National publicity

You Asked For It, the popular television show hosted by Art Baker, once featured Little Tyke. The producers wanted a scene with chickens, which didn't bother Georges since Little Tyke roamed easily among chickens at Hidden Valley Ranch. When the film crew brought the chickens in, they turned out to be four little day-old chicks!

Slurp of the tongue

Little Tyke's only previous experience with new chicks had been with a hen and her chicks who had wondered onto the lawns around their home on the ranch. Georges thought nothing of it until he saw Little Tyke acting peculiarly, slinking into the house, and looking guilty with lips tightly closed over obviously open jaws. He called, "Tyke! What have you got?" Instantly her mouth opened and a little chick popped out, unharmed. Flapping its little down-covered wings, it almost flew back to its upset mother. Apparently Little Tyke had affectionately licked the tiny chick, as she was prone to do when, with one huge slurp of the tongue, the little chick had popped into her mouth, and she hadn't known how to fondle it further!

With the amazed camera crew filming, Little Tyke strode over to the chicks, hesitated long enough to lick the chicks *carefully* and *gently* with the very *tip* of her tongue, and moved away with a yawn. A moment later she came back to lie down among the chicks. They immediately made their way into the long silky hair at the base of her great neck where they peered out from the shelter of their great protector.

Another scene saw a new kitten, after an introduction, walk over to Little Tyke's huge foreleg and sit down. Little Tyke crooked one paw around the tiny creature and cuddled it closer.

In front of cameras, Art Baker picked up a *Bible* and read: "The wolf and the lamb shall feed together, and the lion shall eat straw like the bullock."

Mail poured into the producers, making this episode one of the most popular in the show's history.

Little Tyke's death

Unfortunately, while spending three weeks in Hollywood for the show, Little Tyke contracted virus pneumonia, a disease that took her life a few weeks later. The sudden change in climate may have been a contributing factor. She succumbed quietly in her sleep, retiring early after watching television.

Inspiring to this day

Her life is over, but her teachings live on. Of the many lessons she taught, not the least is that love removes fear and savagery. Little Tyke reflected the love and care shown to her after the first few moments of her precarious birth.

Thousands saw photographs of her lying with her lamb friend, Becky, inspiring many to see the world a fresh way: two such diverse natures enjoying each other's love! One eminent attorney kept a huge enlargement of this photograph in his office, and pointed to it as he counciled couples on the verge of divorce.

Scientific dilemma

Science is at a loss when it comes to Little Tyke. Felines are the strictest of carnivores. Without flesh she should have developed blindness, and dilated cardiomyopathy (DCM), a degenerative disease that turns heart muscles flabby, limiting their ability to pump blood. This is because her diet didn't contain an adequate source of taurine.

Not known to be essential in the 1950s, research at UC Davis in 1976 proved that taurine is an essential nutrient for felines, the lack of which would cause degeneration of the retina. Later research implicated inadequate taurine levels in dilated cardiomyopathy as well. For cats with DCM, if the disease has not progressed too far, administering taurine causes an almost miraculous recovery. Formerly, cats lived only a few days to weeks after diagnoses.

Taurine is non-existent in natural non-animal sources. It is present in minute amounts in milk and eggs. Little Tyke *could* have gotten her taurine requirement from milk, *if* she drank 500 gallons per day, or from eggs, *if* she ate more than 4000 per day. How *did* Little Tyke get taurine?

Challenge

Perhaps even more important, why did Little Tyke disown her species' instincts? Little Tyke is a curiosity to the public, aberration to zoologists, anomaly to scientists, and an inspiration to idealists.

Little Tyke wasn't alone. A photograph taken at Allahabad, India in 1936 shows another awesome lioness.

In *Autobiography of a Yogi*, Paramahansa Yogananda wrote:
...Our group left the peaceful hermitage to greet a near-by swami, Krishnananda, a handsome monk with rosy cheeks and impressive shoulders. Reclining near him was a tame lioness. Succumbing to the monk's spiritual charm — not, I am sure, to his powerful physique! — the jungle animal refuses all meat in favor of rice and milk. The swami has taught the tawny-haired beast to utter "Aum" in a deep, attractive growl — a cat devotee!

These vegetarian lionesses are *lion lights*. By example, these luminaries invite us as well to discover a less violent world, turning away from slaughterhouses that fed our dogs and cats prior to this age of enlightenment.

Chapter 2

WHY

Sometimes it helps to put into words just why we want our pets to go vegetarian. When family, friends, and veterinarians ask about reasons, where does one start?

ETHICAL

Animals think, reason, feel pain, hope, raise families, and communicate. Laws protect them from abuse, *except* for farm and research animals, which possess the *same* foregoing attributes. Isn't it a little egotistical to think that animals exists solely for our use or abuse? Specism is another form of racism.

To be or not to be

Congress amended the Animal Welfare Act in 1971 to give humane treatment and care to animals. The U.S. Department of Agriculture, responsible for enforcing the act, *refuses* to define rats, mice and birds as animals, excluding them from this law. What are they, if not animals? Perhaps if mice are defined as animals, cows and chickens may line up next. Wouldn't *that* create a dilemma for those who use and consume animals?

An eye for an eye

Perhaps animal life and plant life *are* equitable. Is a lamb *really* different from a legume? My mother-in-law sent an article from her church's periodical, *Our Sunday Visitor,* entitled, "How many tomatoes gave their lives for that salad?"

Does it bother you pluck out the eyes of a potato, or perhaps eat the eyes with the skin? Is it arrogance that allows us to gnaw on the heart of celery or an ear of corn? ...or a salad, knowing full well that the heads were decapitated from their source of life? Just who do we claim to be in the hierarchy of being that justifies killing vegetables so that we can live?

...I believe in an order of being that allows us humans to eat lower life forms — animals and vegetables. ...I believe that both the Genesis story and human reason allow us to eat of the fruits of the earth, and from the animal kingdom (exclusive of humans).

I do not believe that the animals we eat are equal to us. I do not believe that they have equal rights....

Only we humans have the potential to love each other in ways that others in the animal kingdom cannot.

Father White, rural-life director the Archdiocese of Dubuque, Iowa, challenges:

...But extremists like PETA and other animal "rightists" really get under my skin. This "ex-couch potato" will take a stand with them, however, if they can look me "in the eye" and give me their justification for killing insects so that they can shred to pieces heads of cabbage and lettuce and eat the hearts out of celery.

A child will lead

Think of the child from *The Emperor's New Clothes,* who saw the foolish naked man and shouted, "He's wearing no clothes!"

Another child laughs, pulling up radishes, but cries at a rabbit's slaughter. Isn't childlike just being sensitive — being able to *see?*

The *Bible* says, "The wolf also shall dwell with the lamb, and the leopard shall lie down with the kid; and the calf and the young lion …together; and a little child shall lead them." Lead in what? In context it seems *not eating animals.*

Abandoning his inner child, Father White sees no difference between head of lamb and head of lettuce. He justifies consuming animals by saying animals can't love others in the ways humans can. He has never seen the mourning rites of chimpanzees or dogs staying long years by the burial sites of their former masters. Animals love unconditionally without "people games."

Fernand Mery once said:

With the qualities of cleanliness, discretion, affection, patience, dignity, and courage that cats have, how many of us, I ask you, would be capable of being cats?

I remember pulling weeds in the backyard, listening to the Dodgers play baseball, with Princess (my dog) next to me. Over by the big redwood fence, caged rabbits panted in the heat.

Innocence lost

As a 13-year-old, Dad showed me how to hold a rabbit's ears with one hand while the other lifted the hatchet. When I did it, the hatchet struck two blows, one to my heart, making killing animals impossible from that moment on.

The memory still haunts me. Dinner that night I passed over rabbit, and ate potatoes and corn. Years would pass before I embraced vegetarianism, but I never touched rabbit again.

Brainwashing

Conditioning starts in infancy. Reinforced with billions of red stained dollars it equates chick peas with chickens. It creates unexamined values, *"Food* animals do not have rights of other animals."

Tara Spreadborough broke through layers of conditioning when she wrote us from California:

> Right now I have 13 cats and two dogs. I couldn't really figure out: if I want to save animals, than why am I feeding them to my animals.

Murder under any other name is still...

Allegedly killed as humanely as possible, San Francisco's 500 ceremonial sacrifices each year upset some people, although mostly chickens are killed, and eaten afterwards. In supporting a proposed ban, the county supervisor stated, "Frankly, even if it is consumed, we still object to the *murder* of animals."

Our local newspaper's "Sheriff's Reports," reported that a neighbor's chickens had been shot at by a BB gun. One chicken was reported "murdered." Commercial food companies legally kill billions and call it "processing." What's the difference?

Regarding respect

It's easier now, in my twenty-third year without meat, articulating seeds planted long ago. Eating with respect for higher (more complex) forms of life means choosing vegetarianism.

Murder is the most nefarious criminal offense and killing animals most human-like is next. In this hierarchy, animal life is before plant life. Too, compare *violence* in killing animals versus plants. What animal *tries* to get eaten? Threatened, they scamper, spring, soar, swim and slither away. Plants patiently wait, tempting us with their exquisitely colored and scented succulent fruits.

Veterinarian support

David Jaggar completed his training in veterinary medicine and surgery at the University of Edinburgh (England) in 1965.

He worked in general practice in England and later for the U.S. Department of Agriculture, before taking a position on the faculty in the College of Medicine at the University of Cincinnati.

His veterinary work brought him in contact with animals used in research, livestock, horses in various equestrian sports, and companion animals as pets. The degree of animal suffering and exploitation appalled him.

While not rejecting the benefits of western medicine, especially in first aid and emergency care, he explores less generally accepted approaches to veterinary health care, including acupuncture, nutrition, herbal medicine, homeopathy, and chiropractic. He is a founding member and past president of the International Veterinary Acupuncture Society. In the *Vegepet Gazette* he wrote:

...However, many holistic veterinarians remain skeptical about not providing flesh foods to meet the biologically evolved carnivorous behavior of cats. One outspoken veterinarian even suggested it was a violation of cats' rights.

An enormous quantity of information is available regarding the nutritional needs of cats. I see no reason why it should violate their rights to satisfy these needs from non-animal sources. It is notoriously difficult to provide a firm philosophical foundation for assertions about animal rights, but making it possible for cats to be vegetarian is surely no greater violation of animal rights than:

1) domesticating cats and preventing them from hunting their own food

2) killing literally millions of chickens, cattle, sheep, horses, fish, etc., to feed domestic pets

It is hard to see how cats have a right to eat the flesh of animals such as those listed above, when this flesh would never form a part of a feral or wild cat's diet. Moreover, since this flesh has often been condemned as contaminated or unfit for human consumption, deliberately feeding it to cats threatens their health and is closer to a violation of than a promotion of cats' rights.

People feeding cats a vegetarian diet are also open to the charge that they are "playing god" to the extent that they are confronting the biological evolutionary path of cats to be carnivorous and to be meddling with "nature" like those involved with the recent trends in genetic technology. However, there is nothing that is strictly natural in any sense that means it is independent from human behavior and observation — which certainly have effects on everything living on this planet.

Cats, like us, also have a cultural evolutionary dimension to their existence, even if less developed than our own. Cultural evolution occurs at a far greater speed than biological evolution. We have the capacity (and some would say responsibility) to decide what kind of human beings we want to become. If we decide to "exploit" cats as pets, then we take on the responsibilities of our relationship to them.

Cats are quite adaptable, as we have discovered. They have the capacity to adapt to humans in a variety of ways. So, rather than "playing god," I see some humans and cats evolving a new kind of cultural evolution path and relationship that has the potential to lead to much less suffering in the world, a more cooperative relationship between humans and the non-human world, and more consideration being given to cats' health than that provided by those who collude with the primarily profit-motivated conventional commercial pet food industry.

The need to reduce animal suffering is urgent. Killing several species of animals to feed cats (and dogs) can no longer be justified now that nutritious alternative diets are economically and conveniently available.

Prey for friends

A client asked Michael W. Fox, America's best known animal psychologist, how long chipmunks live. He wrote in *Understanding Your Cat*:

> ...Since they are preyed on by owls, stoats, foxes, and so on, they produce many young, but few survive longer than

two or three years. Living for seven years in captivity must be a record.

As for your fifteen-year-old cat that brought the chipmunk home as an infant to play with, and still plays with it — it supports one of my main beliefs: Pets need pets, and provided no one is frustrated and deprived of security, food and affection, prey and predator, mouse and lion, can, and will, live peacefully together.

Getting the meat out

I was so excited to know I could feed Holly, my miniature Schnauzer, a wholesome vegetarian meal. We have absolutely no meat or eggs in our home — for pets or people.

Elizabeth Trowley — Michigan

Feeding our cat, until now, has been the last link with the slaughterhouse. We're very glad to be able to finally break that link!

Susan Moloney — Connecticut

Thanks for your wonderful product! It turned a stray cat on the verge of starvation into a beautiful animal (much to the surprise of our vet), and all this without sacrificing my ethics.

Alison Shepard — Florida

Darlene Boord from California called her discovery of *Vegecat* "one of the most important things in my life." She went on:

Always before I was in a dilemma: Should I give my support to the slaughterhouse industry by hiring them to kill animals for me to feed to my beasts? Or should I cause injury to my own beloved beasts by feeding them food that was inadequate nutritionally?

I believe it is wrong to injure those close to you in the name of helping some nameless, faceless throngs somewhere else. If you don't do right by those close to you, how can you hope to do right for anybody else? So I felt I had to keep buying that awful cat food for my loved ones. However, now that I've discovered *Vegecat*, I just feel so good about not having to cause death or suffering for anybody.

Leaders don't always lead

Active in the animal rights movement, Darlene shared her disappointment with some leaders who seem closed-minded when it comes to feeding their own pets, blemishing their otherwise exemplary lives:

My own experiences in talking with people who supposedly care about all these issues has been somewhat disappointing. Even [—] was heard to say that his cat didn't like it and so he didn't make him eat it. I find that amazing. I feel that if you're a public person who stands for veganism and animal rights and so forth, especially one who goes around preaching all the time, you should be an example for others, not the weakest of the lot. Where are his priorities? What's more important — making sure your cat doesn't have to eat what he doesn't prefer, or stopping the torture and killing of innocent beasts? [—] recently said to me on the phone that feeding her dogs a vegetarian diet was more costly and more time consumptive and that's why she didn't do it. I ask you, isn't stopping the slaughter an important enough issue for us to spend a little extra time and a little extra money? (Besides, I don't think it's any more costly at all.) It's just very disappointing when leaders talk and act this way.

Companions on the path

My cat is now a vegetarian — thank you for your help. I am on a spiritual path that requires all of our animals as well as ourselves to be vegetarian.   Ann Waters — California

Everyone who has loved, and been loved by a dog or cat realizes the depths of love and faithfulness possible. No longer do strict vegetarian households have to lose out on this wonderful experience because of dietary concerns.

If it were not for you and the availability of your product, allowing us to provide our cat with a vegan diet, we would not have accepted the opportunity to adopt her and would have missed out on knowing and loving this fabulous fellow being.

Joanne Stepaniak — Pennsylvania

...I had always avoided cat ownership because I believed it would be impossible to feed a cat a non-meat diet.

When I found Rudy, she was just a baby kitten, who had been abandoned on a rural highway. She was so tiny and so ill that the veterinarian was not sure that she would survive. Having found this helpless creature, I was faced with a dilemma. I could not bring myself to purchase pet food that was manufactured at the expense of other animals, and yet I could not turn my back on this precious kitten who so desperately needed care and nourishment.

Luckily, I remembered having heard about *Vegekit.*

Rudy is now almost one year old and perfectly healthy and happy. She enjoys the Oat-Soy recipe that I can make in about 10 minutes and store in the refrigerator. There is no repulsive smell at feeding time, and the yeast in the recipe appears to repel fleas and ticks so that they are not a problem, in spite of the fact that we live in the country. Furthermore, Rudy appears to truly relish and anxiously anticipate the taste of her meals.

Thanks so much for making possible for me to cherish my friendship with Rudy without having to compromise my commitment to a nonviolent lifestyle.

Carol Arens — Arkansas

Dog eat dog

Animal shelters in 1984 killed more than 20,000,000 unwanted pets, at an average weight of 40 pounds per pet (pet-cemetery industry figure). Veterinarians euthanatized an additional 10,000,000 pets, creating a disposal problem of 600,000 tons.

Increasingly, landfills and incinerators refuse animal bodies, but one major option remains, and this *makes* instead of *costs* money. Rendering plants recycle carcasses into pet food by sending animal bodies through a hammer-mill, crushing bones and chopping carcasses. Mixed with animal wastes from slaughterhouses it is now called "meat by-products," and sold to pet food producers.

According to a 1973 *Chicago Tribune* report, a pet food company spokesman confirmed that 15 percent of dry pet food consists of rendering company by-products. Today, pet food companies buy from many small rendering plants, and it is difficult to get accurate figures as to what percentage is dog and cat. Rendering companies understandably are close mouthed. John Eckhouse, of the *San Francisco Chronicle,* reported that executives at one plant, Modesto Tallow, denied they even picked up pets. Yet employees, vendors and state inspectors said they regularly observed dogs and cats rendered at both their Sacramento and Modesto plants. At Sacramento Rendering, one employee stated, "Thousands and thousands of pounds of dogs and cats are picked up and brought here every day." An ex-employee confirmed, "The small animals are a big part of the company."

Iris Nowell, in her 1978 book *The Dog Crisis,* considered, "This is a valuable and [a] self-replenishing food supply for pets." Going on, she stated:

> The unacceptability of this notion is proportionate to the concept of how human one's dog is. It is the rule rather than the exception to think of the dog as a family member, and because a potent taboo for humans is eating human flesh, the attitude translates readily to the family pet, whose owner sees him as more human than animal. Pet food manufacturers wouldn't bat an eye over using dogs as common materials. ...Their concern is the bottom line and they would no doubt consider it prudent, in exchange for such an economical resource, to throw some of their advertising weight into campaigns to precondition customers to the idea.

Spending money to condition people wasn't necessary after all. Pet food companies, without fanfare, package rendered pets.

ECOLOGICAL

In the USA, pet food manufacturers in 1990 neatly converted more than 2,200,000,000 pounds of cattle, sheep, fish, and chickens into pet food. What is the ecological cost of producing this incredible carnage for America's more than 100,000,000 cats and dogs?

Agricultural engineers at Ohio State University stated: "Even the best of the animal enterprises examined returns only 34.5% of the investment of fossil energy to us in food energy, whereas the poorest of five crop enterprises examined returns 328%."

One hundred pounds of plant protein produces just six pounds of beef. One hundred pounds of plant protein, fed chickens, returns 17 pounds of meat and with pigs the figure drops to 12 pounds.

Eighty-five percent of the 7,000,000,000 tons of topsoil lost in the United States each year directly relates to raising livestock.

If cats and dogs go vegetarian, we save a potential 20 billion pounds of plant protein. How far would that go towards feeding the 60,000,000 people who starved to death last year?

Feeding meat to your pets may no longer be ethically or ecologically justifiable and someday may be prohibitively expensive. Wellness is another aspect.

HEALTH

Oregonian Valyen Turner wrote:

The idea of a vegetarian cat is an admirable — and desirable — one. But my concern is with the health of the animal being fed such a diet over many years. I know you claim that

your diet with the *Vegecat* supplement meets all their requirements. However, I would like to know whether those
people with vegetarian cats have animals who are kept indoors, and whether those animals have been fed vegetarian
meals over a period of two years or more. Any animal who is
allowed out-of-doors for any length of time, whether on a
leash or not, cannot be called vegetarian, and those people
whose animal are out cannot claim a success with a vegetarian diet.

I would like our cats to be vegetarian, but ours are strictly
indoor cats who, moreover, have passed through a serious
liver ailment that still affects them. Their health is a daily
concern. It is unethical for me to use them as trial animals if
the vegetarian diet has not been fed successfully to indoor animals over time.

We can understand this concern. When we began research,
information supporting vegetarian diets for pets (especially cats)
was mostly non-existent. Laboratory trials deplorably sacrifice
animals, and microscopically examine their tissue slices for abnormal signs. Obviously this is unacceptable for us. However,
with more than six years of documented success, we can state that
this method of feeding normally carnivorous animals has exceeded
our fondest hopes.

Annette Savage from Texas wrote:
As always, I am so grateful for the work you have done.
My only hope was that "my" cats would be *as* healthy as be-
fore. I never even imagined that they would be healthier.

18-year-old Melanie has come back to life; Oliver's copper
colored eyes are turning green(!); and Egypt, the wild one, is as
sleek and sassy as ever.

Veterinarians see millions of sick cats and dogs every year, the
vast majority raised and maintained on commercial foods advertised as the latest word in healthy eating. What goes into these pet
foods that makes them so bad?

4-D meat

Pet foods often contain ill defined "by-products." These can contain grade "4-D" meat, defined by the U.S. Department of Agriculture as dead, dying, disabled, and diseased.

Whole mammal bodies (cows, sheep, pigs, etc.) by the hundreds of thousands, millions of their major parts, and thousands of tons of bird flesh end up at the reject pile. Much of this waste is diseased, and often cancerous. Mason and Singer in their book *Animal Factories,* report that cancerous tissues from slaughterhouses average fifteen million pounds a year. This reject pile is soon on the move as it magically changes into "meat meal" and "by-products" on pet food labels.

Dr. Richard H. Pitcairn and his wife Susan writing in *Dr. Pitcairn's Complete Guide to Natural Health for Dogs and Cats* state:

> From his experience as a veterinarian and federal meat inspector, Dr. P. F. McGargle concludes that feeding slaughterhouse wastes to animals increases their chances of getting cancer and other degenerative disease...

> ...Furthermore, the increase in cancer rates corresponds to the introduction and increased use of meat meal as an animal food.

Something fishy

A recent *Consumers Report* article made waves by concluding that fish are dangerous. Of their samples of *people* quality fish, 43 percent of the salmon contained PCBs, and 90 percent of the swordfish contained mercury. Since fish is one of the most perishable of all foods, 40 percent had bacteria counts higher than 500,000 per gram, indicative of spoilage, and 30 percent contained 10 million or more, meaning rotten. Fish ending up in pet food is even worse.

According to John Robbins in his laudable book, *Diet For A New America:*

Fish have a remarkable ability to absorb and concentrate toxic chemicals from their watery environments. For one thing, their food chains are extremely long, with phytoplankton being eaten by zooplankton, who are in turn eaten by tiny fish, who are then eaten by larger fish, and so on. More significantly, fish literally breathe the water they swim in, so they are also continually accumulating more and more contaminants in this manner. The net effect is almost as if they were underwater magnets for toxic chemicals. The EPA [Environmental Protection Agency] estimates fish can accumulate up to nine million times the level of PCBs in the waters in which they live!

Plus additives

Not only do most commercial pet foods support factory farming, supply nutrients of tainted value, but they may in addition contain additives of questionable safety. BHA is practically universal and additives not permitted in food for humans show up in pet food.

Improved fur

Anitra Frazier, in her early years as a concerned groomer, had her clients add yeast and bran to their cats' meals. We don't advocate adding bran because of its magnesium content, but she definitely saw big changes when she saw the cats again. She found startling improvements in their coats — changes she called *incredible.* Oily coats were less oily, and dull coats became silky. That began her interest in better nutrition for cats that resulted in her publishing *The Natural Cat* in 1981. She states in its 1990 incarnation, *The New Natural Cat:*

Then I begin to notice that cats whose health was below par did not show the change in coat quality as dramatically. Therefore, I reasoned, coat quality seems to be a barometer of the internal health of the cat. ...Sixteen years and several hundred cats later, I can honestly say that I was right.

Many letters and pictures we've received illustrate this. Betty Zukov from California wrote:

My seventeen-year-old dog's fur has doubled in length since I put her on the *Vegedog* diet. By this, I mean it is twice as long as it ever was, even when she was much younger.

My dogs have been eating home-cooked food for some years, but I was using a different formula that required meat. I am so happy to be able at last to completely eliminate meat from my home.

Alison Shepard wrote us about his two dogs, who aren't troubled with coat problems:

VANYA & VLADIMIR

Vanya (age 10) and her son, Vladimir (age 5) have always been vegetarian. Since we're going to breed Vladimir, we had his hips X-rayed for certification. He got "excellent" rating from O.F.A. — top score!

He and his mom have beautiful coats and skin. Here in Florida, skin problems are very common — hot spots, etc. Also, they don't seem to attract fleas. People assume we "bomb" our house & soak our yard with pesticides, like everyone else seems to. They can't believe the answer is diet.

Les & Susan Stewart from California wrote about how their cat, Dancer, improved with the addition of *Vegecat* (we *don't* recommend calcium magnesium powder):

Thank you so much for *Dogs & Cats Go Vegetarian* and *Vegecat* — we think you saved our cat, Dancer's life.

For the last seven years (ever since we first got Dancer at age five months) we had been feeding him a vegetarian diet — supplemented with powered mix (kelp, lecithin, brewer's yeast, calcium/magnesium powder). We were under the impression that he was getting the taurine he needed in the raw eggs and cheese we gave him. He was outdoors during the day — we know he raided garbage cans and did some hunting.

About a year ago, we moved and Dancer became an indoor cat by choice. Within a few months, we noticed him sleeping most of the day, lethargic and uninterested in much of anything, not eating very well — and to our horror, he had lost nearly three pounds of his nine and one-half pounds normal weight. About the time we observed this I had received your book, *Dogs & Cats Go Vegetarian*, and had started to read it.

After adding a taurine supplement (I guessed on the amount as I could not find any information on how much cats need) at first and then changing his diet and adding *Vegecat*, we are happy to say that he regained his weight and is playful and interested in life again!

We are vegans and are so grateful to find a healthful way of feeding our cat without contributing to the slaughter of other innocent creatures.

Legendary Blue Cats of France

Katherine Kisrow, proprietor of Velure Cattery in Tennessee, wrote:

I have just recently begun using your pet food supplements, with more initial success than I dreamed possible! In addition to my mixed-breed household pets, I have a small colony of purebred Chartreux cats, the oldest natural breed of domestic feline in the world. Ironically, these beautiful animals were at one time hunted for their pelts and their *meat*.

I had sought after a vegetarian diet for my cats for years, but, like everyone else, constantly ran up against a brick wall. I was excited to learn of Barbara Peden's book through *Vegetarian Times*, and I immediately ordered some *Vegecat*. Though some of my brood are still holding out for their kibbles, many (especially the younger ones not yet set in their ways) flock around when they see me get out the mixing bowl. I've had great fun with the recipes in the book, and now understand the proportions well enough to make up some of my own. The cats on the diet are really thriving so far. In fact, at a cat show this past weekend, one of my kittens received a "Best Kitten in Show" award. The judge remarked on his excellent condition, and I was very proud to announce that he is a vegetarian!

Though the word "breeder" tends to have a bad connotation these days, I believe, as in all walks of life, there are "good" ones and "bad" ones. The good ones breed with respect and intelligence, producing kittens in moderate numbers. Cat shows draw many spectators, and provide a wonderful opportunity to cultivate love and understanding of all cats, and to educate on matters of proper care, humane issues, etc. I will be most happy to endorse and recommend *Vegecat* at shows, to kitten buyers and whenever possible, if you don't mind a "breeder" doing so.

We were pleased to hear more from Katherine when she wrote us the following letter:

I am still experiencing success using *Vegepet* supplements in my cattery, and am enclosing a couple of "testimonial" type photographs. One is of Velure Gelfling, a Chartreux female kitten whom we affectionately nicknamed "Itty Bitty Kitty Witty!" Her mom's milk ran out when she was but four weeks old (most Chartreux don't

ITTY BITTY KITTY WITTY

complete the weaning process until eight to ten weeks) and due to her small size, I feared she would not survive. I tried giving her some *Vegecat* recipe I made and blended into a gruel, and she loved it! She began to grow and prosper, and I was happy to make her the "flower girl" at my wedding!

The second photo [not shown] is of Velure Eden, being looked over by CFA judge Wain Harding at the Pro/Plan CFA Invitational Cat Show held in Dallas, Texas in November [1991]. Although the show was sponsored by Purina(!), I made sure to bring Eden's favorite *Vegecat* recipe (I have found that for traveling, since lack of refrigeration is a problem, I can mix dry ingredients and carry jars of organic baby food — like *Earth's Best* — then combine the two at mealtime.) Eden was Best Chartreux Premier in Show. (I might add that I use Purina *Rabbit Chow* in my litter boxes, a much healthier alternative to conventional clay litter.)

At a recent after-show part attended by cat breeders, the subject of diet cropped up. When I stated that a large portion of my cats' rations are homemade, the first words out of another breeder's mouth were, "That's bad." How sad that it is automatically assumed that something we make with our own hands, knowing the source of each ingredient, is automatically inferior to some uniform looking brown pellets that come in a fancy wrapper. How trusting we are, or how easily duped... I do have to admit that I still use some of those brown pellets in my cattery for the sake of convenience, and so that those cats and kits who are eventually adopted into other homes can easily make the transition. That's okay... the "New Age" is coming...

Chapter 3

BEST IS

FRESH

reshly prepared, carefully selected food is superior to canned, dried, extruded, colored, artificially flavored, and preserved food. Food processors want us to believe otherwise.

Pet food not only contains, but *is* the proverbial sacred cow for many companies. In 1991, excluding pet stores and veterinarians, commercial dog foods sold in the United States amounted to $3,910,000,000. Commercial cat foods amounted to another $2,491,000,00, totaling over 6 billion, 400 million dollars to feed America's 54 million dogs and 62 million cats! Pet shops and veterinarians rang up another billion dollars. This information is from the $1000 per copy *Maxwell Report,* eagerly bought by major rollers in this game of high stakes. Appendix 1 takes a revealing look at the pet food industry.

One of the strongest *opponents* of using fresh foods is Dr. Francis Kallfelz, professor of clinical nutrition at the New York State College of Veterinary Medicine, Cornell University and well-known columnist for *Cat Fancy* magazine.

Asked if pet owners should be encouraged to add fresh foods to pets diets, he responded in *Petfood Industry* magazine:

As long as they are feeding a complete and balanced diet, there is no need to add fresh foods to a dog's or a cat's diet. As far as I'm concerned, there's no objective evidence to prove there are any beneficial effects of that practice.

When asked if he *objected* to fresh foods he replied:

No, not necessarily. As long as you don't add more than 10%, by weight, to a pet's diet. It probably won't hurt, because there's enough of a safety factor built into pet foods to offset it. But, I've seen no proof that there is any nutritional benefit to doing so.

Dr. Kallfelz's budget is dependent to a large extent upon grants from pet food companies. Is this the prompting that guides his apparent ignorance?

Pottenger's cats

Between the years 1932 to 1942, Francis Pottenger, Jr. conducted a feeding experiment involving *900* cats to determine the effects of fresh as opposed to cooked food. As unpalatable as research that sacrifices cats is, nonetheless it's valuable to learn what we can.

His carefully documented work, most recently published in 1983 as *Pottenger's Cats,* fills a 126 page book with charts and photos.

The *cooked* food group of cats were irritable, tormented by vermin and intestinal parasites, suffered skin lesions, allergies, heart, kidney and liver problems, bad eyesight, infections of glands, joint and nervous disorders. By the third deficient generation, none survived past the sixth month of life, diarrhea followed by pneumonia being the principal cause of death.

The raw food group of cats suffered none of the preceding ailments. The food in both groups, although essentially the same, was cooked in one group and uncooked in the other. Pottenger could only speculate what vital elements found only in raw food were missing when cooked. Tissue enzymes are unstable in heat, as well as some vitamins, but his research took him to other fields. However, his carefully documented study of raw versus cooked food has great significance in formulating diets.

Dr. Pottenger's work is frequently quoted by others, yet Kallfelz reports that, *"there's no objective evidence…"* He also takes a swipe at those who advocate natural pet foods:

Natural pet foods provide no nutritional advantages when compared with conventional pet foods. The actual nutrient levels of both types of food are similar. In fact, "natural" foods have several disadvantages: Increased price, poorly protected fat and the presence of poorly defined substances.

The absence of synthetic antioxidants may result in rancidity of the fat, which could cause serious clinical consequences, particularly to cats. The labels of some "natural" pet foods claim that additional vitamin E has been added to their products as a natural antioxidant. Unless, however, this is added at the time the fat is refined, vitamin E may be ineffective because this vitamin prevents the process of rancidity but does not reverse it. Although vitamin E is less toxic than other fat-soluble vitamins, it can still be toxic at high levels. How much are they adding?

Kallfelz should know that food processors put as little vitamin E in their formulations as possible since it is one of their most costly ingredients. It is *not* considered toxic, although extraordinarily high amounts can cause loss of appetite as well as slightly impaired blood coagulation. He continues:

Additives such as comfrey, rosemary, hydrangea, raspberry leaves and dried kelp, are sometimes found in the ingredients list of "natural" pet foods. These substances are added apparently because of their hypothetical nutritional or "health giving" properties. However, I have yet to find any objective scientific evidence to prove the benefits of such substances as dried kelp and comfrey. Rather, I have found scientific evidence to contrary. The chemical content of any such natural product is likely to be quite variable. Also, deleterious chemicals may be present in some of these products. I would never feed my dog pet foods containing such undefined substances, nor would I recommend them to my clients.

Apparently he has *not* investigated the properties of kelp. Factories located in the United States, Nova Scotia, Eire, Scotland, France, Denmark, the Netherlands, Norway, and South Africa manufacture animal feed from brown alga (seaweed).

A Norwegian factory harvests ascophyllum nodosum, dries it in the sun, removes excess salt, and caramelizes the sugar content to eliminate an odor repellent to cattle and horses. The meal made from this process is claimed to have a food value equal to that of oats, prevent or cure mineral deficiency diseases, and results in "better milk, eggs, meat, and fur."

Dr. Kallfelz wouldn't have to go far to research kelp. Professor Cavanaugh, at the same Cornell University resident to Dr. Kallfelz, published research establishing kelp's efficacy upon fractures. In *Seaweed and Vitality*, John Zorn writes:

Studies were made of the blood calcium, phosphorus, iron, and iodine on patients with fractures at different intervals during convalescence. Professor Cavanaugh learned that the healing time of fractures was reduced 20% by giving the patient a daily ration of kelp. Accordingly, it was clearly indicated in the study that kelp raised the level of calcium in the blood.

Mark Morris, Jr., Research Vice President of Morris Animal Foundation, is responsible for much nutritional information that guides legitimate pet food companies. One reason he objects to natural foods is that they don't have a long shelf life, a critical key for profitable marketing. In *Petfood Industry* he wrote:

> The whole area of natural foods is certainly a noteworthy controversy. My feeling is that, if in order to offer a natural product, I'm required to eliminate things that are beneficial to the product — its keeping ability, shelf life, etc. — then I don't want the natural product.
>
> ...I think the data showing the benefit of adding fresh foods is lacking. Whether or not you see a response is going to depend upon the quality of the base diet that you're supplementing. The use of fresh foods can be very insidious....

Experts advise fresh

Note Morris's concern about benefits to the *product* — no mention about benefits to the animal. With eyes glued to the microscope, he sees fresh foods as a *threat*. Leaving him there, hear Randy Wysong, founder of the Wysong Institute, (a non-profit research, educational and ecologically active organization), and of the "natural is better" school. He wrote in *Petfood Industry:*

> Pet owners should include fresh foods in their pets' diets. Science is not at the end point that the "100% complete" diet claim implies. The pet food industry and regulatory agencies should concede this fact and quit pretending.

Identifying with parents he says:

> ...How many parents would take the advice of a pediatrician who placed a packaged food product on the exam table and told the parent that this is the only product they should feed the child day-in, day-out, for the child's lifetime, and further that they should be sure to not feed any other foods because that might unbalance the product? Even if the pediatrician gave assurances of nutrient analyses that exceed required minimum levels, feeding trials, and even if

the label guaranteed "100% complete and balanced," how many parents would accept such counsel?

The suggestion seems absurd. Surely a child should not go without eating fresh apples, carrots and home-cooked meals. We intuitively know that which is plucked from the vine, so to speak, is better and likely more healthful than processed and packaged products embalmed with various additives to increase shelf life.

Although it seems unreasonable, even ridiculous in the human parallel, such recommendations for pet food are a way of life for veterinarians, academia, government and industry. Thus that which is absurd in human nutrition has become commonplace, expected, and even mandated in pet nutrition.

...Food variety and the incorporation of fresh food products in the daily diet are the cornerstones to good human nutrition. ...We don't have complete knowledge of what nutrients a pet requires. Dietary variety, not relying on one processed food, is the key to preventing dietary deficiency.

...Subtle nutritional problems can predispose to overt disease, but the cause may be far removed, in time, from the effect, so a nutritional problem may never be suspected. For example, how does one set out to prove or disprove that the pancreatic cancer occurring in a 10-year-old dog is or is not the result of feeding a manufactured "100% complete" diet for the life of the animal?

Processing can decrease nutrient content and bioavailability and create new toxic compounds that are potentially carcinogenic, mutagenic, atherogenic, and free radical generating. ...Processing changes often do not result in effects that can be seen in short-term feeding trials and are usually not seen in digestibility studies. Nevertheless, these subtle biochemical changes are important, if not critical, in terms of evaluating the long-term nutritional value of any food.

...The public should be encouraged to supplement their pet's diet with fresh foods and be educated as to how to do so.

In *Understanding Your Cat*, Michael Fox relates:

I have a castrated male Abyssinian — I give him Purina chow and every other day a moist canned food, table scraps (he loves corn on the cob and bananas), and grass (lawn, that is). Diversity of diet, but a balanced diet, is a safe rule.

Campfire cats

Anitra Frazier adds:

Cats in the wild don't build a campfire and toast their mouse like a marshmallow. When food is cooked, both vitamins and enzymes are destroyed. Also, the fat and protein molecules can be altered by the heating process, making it more difficult for the cat's system to digest and use them.

If you decide to use a commercial canned food (containing *no fish*) as part of your cat's diet, you can supplement that food with some of the missing elements — once you are aware of what those elements are.

The first is *freshness.* Living in a natural state, the cat would eat nothing but food that was alive just one second before it was eaten. The Kirlian experiments carried out in both the U.S.S.R. and here have used special light waves to photograph the vital life force in living organisms which is gradually lost when the organism dies. Obviously this vital force is no longer present in a container on the grocery store shelf or even in our own cooked table food. To replace this vital force, you can add a raw organic egg yolk three times a week and a teaspoon of finely grated raw carrots, chopped alfalfa sprouts, or fresh chopped chives once a day to the cat's food.

Wendell Belfield lambastes commercial pet foods:

Despite industry claims that pets live long and healthy lives on commercial pet food, we veterinarians are routinely faced with contradictory evidence in the form of sick animals. We frequently encounter acute reactions such as diarrhea and vomiting and skin lesions. Most often, though, we are witnessing symptoms of deteriorating health, of diminished efficiency of bodily functions and organs, of kidneys failing in middle age due to excessive protein, of weakened immune

systems and allergic reactions. We are seeing the cumulative
effect of all those additives, toxins, lead, and the very questionable source of the natural ingredients.

Belfield goes on to talk about the importance of some raw
food in the diet, drawing attention to Dr. Pottenger's well known
research with 900 cats. He adds:

Feed your cat table scraps. I have always been an advocate
of this. By table scraps, I don't mean sugar and sweet stuff or
cakes and cookies. I mean meat and vegetables, salad and
cooked cereal....

The pet food industry has tried to discourage people from
feeding their animals from the table, probably because they
don't want anything cutting into their sales. The manufacturers want you to believe your animals are getting all the nutrition they need out of the bag or can. But that's not so.

David Jaggar continues:

Many of us in the holistic veterinary medical field recognize the harmful effects of regular commercial cat foods,
formal veterinary education and company promotions notwithstanding.

Our emphasis is definitely on feeding freshly prepared
meals to cats, both for the cats' health and to foster a more
responsible attitude and an improved quality in the relationship between caretakers and their cats.

Richard Pitcairn recommends including some fresh food
along with the meals of commercial foods, *if* the pet owner de-
cides to use commercial foods. He advises the addition of sprouts,
raw grated carrots, raw eggs and meat scraps. His main thrust is to
start from scratch, and prepare homemade foods for pets. Much
of his book he devotes to making meals for cats and dogs as simple and affordable as possible. Although a vegetarian, he did not
find a workable vegetarian diet for cats. Our research was yet
three years in the future when he and his wife Susan published
their book in 1982.

He quotes a lady in New York who told him:

I have an eight-year-old mixed breed... He weighs about 90 pounds and is magnificent, both in looks and health. He's never had a bath and yet his coat glistens and has no odor. Also his teeth are strong and pure white. ...Buck is about the healthiest dog I've ever known.

His diet is probably no more expensive than commercial food except for the chuck, and I guess some pet owners don't want the extra work of preparation. They should know the small investment in time and money is well worth the effort. They have vet bills — I do not.

Friends think I'm nuts to cook for a dog. They have younger dogs with loose or missing teeth, severe rashes, heart and breathing problems, overweight, lethargy, etc. They say Buck is so healthy because he's a mutt. That might help, but I think the diet and care he gets is part of it also. Buck has never had fleas either.

Disappearing cataracts

Soon after we published our first book, John Grauer of New York wrote us about fresh foods making a difference:

I want to tell you a little story about my dog Simone who will be 16 in July. A couple years ago, she had cataracts — her eyes were cloudy and dull.

Recently, I have been giving her some of my own food (pea soup, tomatoes, cabbage, etc.). I always noticed that after giving her vegetables, her eyes would turn a deeper color brown. Finally, I began to realize that her eyes were not turning color, rather, the cataracts were going away! I haven't been to my vet in a while, but when I go again, I will ask him to look at her eyes. Now they are bright and clear, as far as I can tell.

Actually, I think what did the trick was the cabbage. Simone eats cabbage like there is no tomorrow. She eats it raw, cooked, the cores, any old part of a cabbage. She always wants it, even after she has had her regular dinner! To me, it is kind of funny to see a dog eating cabbage, but that is what she likes (I like it too).

FAMILY MEMBERS

Several years ago, when anemic computers depended partially on type-in programs for their wizardry, I found a listing for a word-search puzzle generator. Before tackling the 20x20 letter grid I first tested a smaller 10x10 letter grid. My daughter, Prema Rose, was home from kindergarten so I made up the smallest possible puzzle, not only to try the new program but also to entertain Rosie. The computer instructed me to enter nine words, from three to seven letters each, and the program would do the rest. I thought, well, how about our family?

I entered all of our names: my wife's, those of our three children, three cat names, our spiritual leader's, and mine. When Rose found that it was a puzzle with our family names as puzzle "pieces," she expressed delight and it turned into a great success.

It got me thinking that many consider their feline friends and canine companions as family members. If you share living space with cats and dogs, you probably harbor these feelings.

According to a survey from Kal Kan (and illustrated on the next page), only 36 percent of the more than 110 million cats and dogs living in America's homes are viewed as "pets." The rest are viewed as family (43 percent) friends (12 percent) children (8 percent), and 1 percent are other (do we really want to know?).

As Dr. Wysong pointed out, how many would feed their children, or other family members or friends, the way they feed their cats and dogs? Fortunately, cats and dogs can have food prepared with the same love and care that benefits the rest of the family.

Family Members

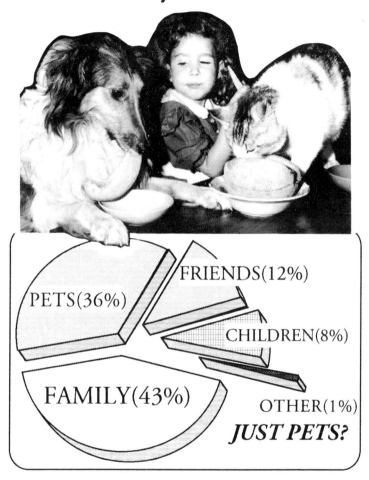

FRIENDS(12%)

PETS(36%)

CHILDREN(8%)

FAMILY(43%)

OTHER(1%)

JUST PETS?

Beyond enzymes

We believe food carries not only vitamins, minerals, enzymes, and other essential nutrients, but also subtle "vibrations" of those who prepare it. In Eastern teachings, these vibrations explain otherwise inexplicable behavior. With home-prepared food, our furry friends harmonize with our vibrations, just as the other members in our families. Isn't this what home is all about?

Chapter 4

THEY ARE
DOING IT

Before our research in 1985-86, publications either discouraged vegetarianism for pets or contained erroneous information. Dogs, being omnivorous, can get their basic needs from plant sources. However, *minimum* nutrient requirement for some nutrients is so high (according to current research), it is almost impossible meeting all requirements on an unsupplemented vegetarian diet.

In the past, irresponsible but well meaning "experts" (without doing the necessary research) encouraged unsupplemented vegetarianism for cats, based upon their personal experiences with a few animals. Apparently health *can* be maintained for dogs, but healthy cats *certainly* supplement their diet with prey (unless natural laws are somehow suspended) — otherwise blindness, heart failure, and other problems result.

Two years after the first edition of *Dogs & Cats Go Vegetarian*, we began publication of the *Vegepet Gazette*. Dedicated to caretakers of vegetarian pets, this newsletter promoted *responsibility*. Available by subscription, it answered commonly asked questions and contained health related articles, veterinarian input and *Vegepet Profiles*.

Speaking from New Hampshire, Mary Currier's boundless enthusiasm for her vegetarian cats and dogs is apparent in this transcript from a recorded interview:

3 DOGS & 13 CATS

HOANA: You have 13 cats and three dogs. Can you tell us about the dogs first?

Mary: Bambi is sort of like a mixed whippet and she's fifteen. And then there is Fox. We got her at a pound and she looks like one of those little Eskimo dogs, but she's mixed. And there's Sheba, also from the pound. She's a golden lab about two years old.

HOANA: And the cats?

Mary: There's Baby; she's about nine. Then there's Butterscotch, she's eight. There's Beautyboat, she's five. Then there's Buffy and Marmalade, and Boopsy, and Amory (she's named for Cleveland Amory) and the mother cat. She's the new addition. Her name is Micha. She has four kittens: Charlie, Rainbow, Scaredicat, and Petunia. And then there's Foofur. She's from Maine. She's just a little kitten too. The kittens have never had anything but the vegetarian food. What they really like, very much, is the garbanzo beans with the egg.

HOANA: Do you use the eggs raw?

Mary: No, I don't. I hard boil them. They seem to like them better when I cook them. They're from free-range hens, too. I buy the garbanzo beans in cans (Progresso brand) and then warm them. I add grated carrot like it says in the book. They really like that.

Sometimes my cat named Amory likes fruit. I tried avocado, like it says in the book, and she was the only one who really loved it. Something else I've been trying (you can only buy it in health food stores) is called seitan [wheat gluten]. They really love that.

HOANA: Isn't that a little expensive for so many cats?

Mary: As long as they eat it I don't care that much about the cost. I mean, if you fed them commercial cat food I think it would be more expensive, besides I wouldn't ever want to do that again.

HOANA: What were they eating before you got *Vegecat*?

Mary: Mainly things like *Fancy Feast, Kal Kan*, and *9 Lives*.

HOANA: How did you make the transition?

Mary: Slowly. They all like these little crunchy foods called *Kitten Chow*. I started moistening that, because I have so many cats, to try to stretch it out. I put a can of cat food in with that. It seemed they didn't like the canned cat food that much, really, they just liked the *Kitten Chow*. So I just added that with the vegetarian food. Then all of a sudden I just stopped completely because they were putting on weight and they were really kind of thin cats. They ate with relish, really! I never saw them eat anything like they do this food! As soon as I have it made they're ready! And they've all gained weight — it's amazing!

HOANA: That's great. So they've gained weight, and they're healthy and happy.

Mary: Their fur is so much softer. It is so much shinier. I sound like a commercial, but I can't believe it, I mean that's how much better off they are. In fact, like I said about my old dog, she was sick. My sons would not go vegetarian at all. They're convinced meat is good for you. They said I was killing the dogs by giving them vegetarian food — that they needed meat. I said, "Well, maybe they're right." You know how you get, like you don't want to be responsible for anything. I stopped feeding the cats anything and just gave them the *Kitten Chow* again, and they wouldn't eat it. Isn't that amazing?

I said, "If Beautyboo eats the vegetarian food," because she was still half and half because of the *Kitten Chow*, "I'll say it's a sign from God that I should stay vegetarian with the cats," and she started gobbling it. She's gained weight, and her fur (black and white) — is gorgeous! All of them, the fur is softer. I don't know what that is. All I can say is what they look like and how they act and they're just so beautiful, all of them.

HOANA: Now the dogs... you say the bark has come back on your older dog?

Mary: Yes! It's the weirdest thing as I was telling my oil man. In fact she saved our home. We have this finished basement and she was barking and the water was coming out of our pipes everywhere all over the basement. I mean, she saved us from a real disaster.

HOANA: Before this she couldn't bark?

Mary: She could not bark. Telling this to the oil man, he said, "What kind of a dog is it?" And I said "vegetarian." *And he just looked at me.* To me it's the only thing different. She didn't bark for two years. She wasn't eating vegetarian before, just the canned dog food.

HOANA: What recipe do you use for the dogs?

Mary: Well, they'll eat them all. Mainly I make them tofu with rice because that seems to be easier. I use *Minute Rice* and add carrots.

HOANA: Going back to the cats for a moment, do the cats get to go outside?

Mary: No, we keep them all inside.

HOANA: So you have a litter box?

Mary: Yes, many!

HOANA: Have you noticed a difference in the odor since changing [their food] from flesh to *Vegecat?*

Mary: Yes, it isn't as bad. It has a different odor.

I'll tell you, though, my dogs, really, I had no problems with them. I had a problem when they were eating dog food. My husband would get down on the floor and pretend he was going to eat it. That's how much they hated dog food. And my husband's so happy that he doesn't have to play any games. In fact, they can hear me mixing the food and they're waiting for it.

HOANA: Did I miss anything?

Mary: If only you could just see these animals and feel the texture of their fur. I think you should put that in because its very important. Their fur doesn't fall out like it used to. It's thicker! It's summer now, and the cats are in the house.

It's amazing. I can't say enough about it and I tell everybody. I'm so grateful.

CATS, CATS, and more CATS

Bernadette Amaker and her mother Barbara have the distinction of having the most experience with vegetarian cats. Since 1986, their cats have consumed well over one hundred large containers of *Vegecat*, each enough to last a cat for almost a year. Since the time of this telephone interview they have adopted even more cats into their Los Angeles home.

HOANA: How many cats do you have?

Bernadette: Nineteen.

HOANA: Do you think you could run through all their names?

Bernadette: In Group A, as we call it, we have Spirit, and Peaceful and then we have two brothers, Light and Life. And then in the group that we call "The Kittens" (who are actually no longer kittens but that's how we identify them), we have a family. We have Zacharias, Jeremiah, and Xoie, and then we have two that are non-related, Sheba and Gloria Esther (who had only one eye when we got her).

And then in Group B (this is the largest group — there are ten in this group) there's Sharon, Daniel, Ezekial (we call him Zeke), David, and we have a family: Joseph is the son, Naomi is the mother, and Rachael Ruth is the daughter. Then we have another family, three sisters: Joanna, Beth Page, and Bethany.

HOANA: When you have families can you just look at them and tell they're related?

Bernadette: The brothers (Light and Life) you can because they look almost identical. The three sisters are all long-haired cats. The two that you would think would be related are the ones that are black and — well, Bethany is more calico. Beth Page is black and has lots of colors in her fur and Joanna is a long-haired orange cat.

So I guess if you tried to figure out which ones are families you would probably automatically pick those two and the three kittens who are related. You can tell two of them definitely because they're almost twins also. Jeremiah is much bigger than Xoie — a big cat.

HOANA: OK, when you group them into Group A and B and so forth is that where they sleep?

Bernadette: Yes, we keep them all separate. We don't mix them. Everybody is separate because it's how we got them.

I spent five hours rescuing some of these cats off a woman's roof in Beverly Hills. Her garage roof was totally overgrown with trees and all kinds of stuff and I stayed up there a total of five hours over two days rescuing them.

HOANA: They were just living up there on their own?

Bernadette: Well, the mother had had kittens and this woman was absolutely terrified of cats, even baby kittens. So she called somebody who called [my] Mom and asked if we could come get these kittens. At the time there were five of them but when we got them (they couldn't have been more than four weeks old if they were that old), the littlest one died soon after, probably of one of those diseases that kittens have. And then one we had put to sleep which was a mistake, because of what the vet said. So then we had those three and then we got Gloria Esther and Sheba and put them in with the group because everybody was so young. We just put them all together.

Light and Life we got together. A lady found them down on the beach, so we refer to them as the "Beach Cats."

The kittens we refer to as "Beverly Hills Cats" because that's where we went to rescue them.

And that's how they're grouped — according to how we got them. We keep them separate. They don't ever get together because in the groups they're in they're fine, but you can get personality conflicts and everything if the groups mix.

HOANA: Have you had them spayed and neutered?

Bernadette: All of them are spayed and neutered.

HOANA: So that really keeps tensions down?

Bernadette: It does except for Zeke who's lately been on — I don't known what's the matter with him. I keep telling him "you don't have any hormones to get worked up with" but he does not believe it.

HOANA: They are all eating vegetarian food?

Bernadette: Oh, absolutely. Definitely. They've been doing that for over three years.

HOANA: Do some of the cats have favorite recipes? Do all of the cats get the exact same food?

Bernadette: They all get the exact same food. Before, they were liking the Tofu and Rice recipe. Then one day it was like everybody had made a collective decision while I slept. The next day I got up to feed them, and I fed them, and nobody ate — anything! I said "this is unusual because we have about four cats who will eat absolutely anything, and nobody ate anything! This is very strange. We're going to have to change — well, I guess they're tired. They've been eating the same thing."

HOANA: Maybe something was wrong with the tofu.

Bernadette: It was all fresh and everything. We even have some who will eat tofu plain. I said, "got to get a new recipe." I got some [canned] garbanzo beans from the store and I opened them up and put them on these little plates and put a little yeast on them and put them all around and everybody ate that. "OK, this will be the next one." So now they're eating their garbanzo beans with the yeast and the *Vegecat* and vegetables and they like that.

HOANA: Well, good. That's what we feed our cats.

Bernadette: But I decided, too, that I'd broaden out their tastes. We had some, even when we had been feeding them before we had changed to *Vegecat.* We had been feeding them dry food and we would wet that and put chopped vegetables in it like we still do. We noticed that some of them have a wide range of tastes, like the two brothers we got from the beach. When we first got them we fed them vegetarian — not quite vegan, because they ate cottage cheese — from the very beginning. They were actually vegetarians for a full year and then I think we got another cat and we couldn't feed them separately. We had to feed them together. So they were eating vegetarian and the others were not, but we figured we had to get everybody together so we put them back on the dry food and then brought them all along together.

This is a sample of what they eat, all of them, and in particular the two brothers: raw mushrooms, avocados, peas, corn, and what is it I found the other day — gluten, they like that. They have a tendency to like Loma Linda products. The brothers used to like bananas and peanut butter, but they don't anymore, but they love cantaloupe and they like watermelon.

HOANA: When we bring cantaloupe into the house we have to hide it because the cats will find it, no matter how high it is. When we eat it we put the rinds out on the lawn and all three cats will clean them down smooth. The smell seems intoxicating to them, they love it so much.

Bernadette: [Laughing] My goodness! Oh, they do love it. That's why I want to try all the others and see who is ready to eat what! It is *something* to see them do that.

HOANA: Raw corn on the cob is the same way. It's fun putting it on the lawn where it doesn't make a mess. They put one foot on it and you can tell they are really enjoying it.

Bernadette: It's so good seeing them eating a variety of things. The last thing was pistachio nuts.

HOANA: Pistachio nuts?

Bernadette: Life particularly loves pistachio nuts.

HOANA: Do you grind them or crush them?

Bernadette: I just break them in half. Life will literally crawl all over your body. I discovered that by accident one day.

    I was standing near the table and I had some pistachio nuts and had no idea that he liked them. He was on the table and walked over to be petted as he usually does, but he smelled these nuts and he just went nuts! He kept grabbing them out of my hand. I couldn't open them fast enough. So then whenever I had them I had to make sure I shelled his portion first so I could eat them peacefully for a little while. He would literally jump on my shoulders and climb all over my body just to get some pistachio nuts and he still does, so that's one of his favorites.

    Also tomatoes — he loves tomatoes. Next I'll try asparagus and some other things and see. But right now they're eating the garbanzo beans and they really like that.

    I found something, just by chance, from Loma Linda that they like. I really like to keep them on the vegetables and everything, but as I say, occasionally it's a nice change of pace for them. They get it every once in a while. Right now they're into Loma Linda's *Tender Rounds*. I gave them some of that today. Oh, cottage cheese — some of them like it, some of them don't.

    When we were changing them over, we figured we would do it on a progression from the dry food (because we never gave them canned food) to the vegetables. We figured we'd go first to fish, then dairy products and then do the *Vegecat* diet. Well, these cats, all of them, never really liked dairy products. They never liked yogurt; never liked milk, never liked cheese except some did go for cottage cheese.

We tried salmon but they didn't like that. We didn't do tuna because everybody warned us against it. They would not eat fish. We were glad of that. We didn't have to go through all those phases. But it was just interesting that they didn't like any of that stuff. When they changed they went from the dry food to the *Vegecat*.

One of the things I like is disproving the fact that cats are strictly carnivores. The other thing is finding out exactly what they do like. We have several of our cats who love gravy. If you give them something with gravy on it they will lick all the gravy off.

HOANA: How do you make your gravy?

Bernadette: We don't make it often because we don't like them to get salt. But there are two things we use.

There is Dr. Bronner's *Balanced-Mineral-Bouillon* that we use which is really good and then there's Bragg's *Liquid Amino.* The Bragg's can be a little salty but on the very, very rare occasions that I make gravy I put it out and say "let's see what they eat." And they like that. That's what I like about this. You go to the store and you say "try it." Bring it home and see if they eat it. It's a nice change of pace and a surprise for them, too.

They love broccoli and spinach — raw spinach. They like to eat the stems. They love that. I had to banish them from the kitchen, because depending upon what group I had out I would be trying to chop up the vegetables and they'd be pulling the broccoli and spinach out of the bowl. It's just incredible the things you discover that they like.

Another thing I noticed when we started to change them over to vegetarian food — the cat boxes didn't smell near as much as they had before!

HOANA: When was the last time you got a new cat?

Bernadette: The last new cat had to be Gloria Esther and that was at least three or four years ago.

HOANA: How would you describe the health of your cats?

Bernadette: They're all pretty healthy. The only on going thing we had was rodent ulcers. The reason they got rodent ulcers is because of the one cat who had it and the doctor said it wasn't contagious. We found out it is. It's a kind of inflammation of the gums. They aren't in any pain. It's called rodent ulcers because it was thought that cats get it from eating mice. We found out that is not the case. It's something that lies dormant in the body and flares up.

HOANA: How many of the cats have it?

Bernadette: Well, everybody had it and I treated them homeopathically so now the only one who really has it is Joseph. He's the one I'm working on now to clear it up.

Zacharia had eczema on the backs of his legs and we took him to the vet and asked him how he would be treated. He said "Oh, eczema's very common among cats, especially on the backs of the legs. It's a classic case." I said, "What are you going to do about it?" He said, "Give him some antihistamines and cortisone." Having been a victim of cortisone myself I said "No, I don't think we're going to do that." So we went back home and I'm the one who studies all the homeopathic books. I said, "well, OK."

I tried some different things and finally settled on graphite. I gave him graphite internally and Mom thought of the graphite cream, which I didn't know was made. So I put that on his legs and it cleared up in about four to six weeks. All the hair's grown back and you would never know that he had eczema. I try to remember to give him graphite once a week because that's what the homeopathic literature says to do for awhile and then you can discontinue it.

HOANA: The homeopathic literature is really for people but you're applying it to cats?

Bernadette: Oh, yes. But as a matter of fact there is a homeopathic materia medica for animals. There are at least a couple of books out. The writing isn't as extensive as it needs to be, but with a lot of work just sitting down and really reading and studying you can apply it.

The thing about homeopathic remedies, and the reason we like them, is that they're proven on people. They're not tested on animals. The man who started it, Hahnemann, had the right idea. If you want to cure people you have to test it on people to find out what happens. That's what he did.

People figured that if this is the reaction it has on people, let's see if we can cure some of the same things that manifest in animals. And sure enough, you can cure almost anything. The materia medica for animals is quite extensive and we use it on the rare occasions that we have to.

When Maria had jaundice before we had changed to this diet we cured her using herbs and homeopathy. We had medicines from the vet but we didn't like doing that because we know medicine is toxic and actually breaks down the body instead of building it up again. So we decided to take a leap of faith and used a book by Pitcairn [*Dr. Pitcairn's Complete Guide to Natural Health for Dogs and Cats*], which is really a good book, and used what he recommended as well as what we knew about herbs and everything. So we used a combination of herbs and homeopathy. The doctor said "Be sure to put her in the window so she'll get lots of sun." And this for a cat who loves to hide in the closet was a pretty tall order. We did all that and, sure enough, she was cleared of her jaundice. And I mean she was really yellow. She was as yellow as a legal pad. That's how yellow she was. But she's cleared up. She's fine.

HOANA: How old are your oldest cats?

Bernadette: That would have to be Life and Light. They are nine. We've had them over eight and one-half years. Gloria Ester is the youngest. The majority of the cats are in the range of five to seven years old.

———————————

In spite of dealing with difficult government officials who zealously protect New Zealand's borders, Ann Macrae Fullerton manages to get *Vegecat* into her country for the benefit of her animals. She penned the following verse in honor of her late Siamese, Melaney:

MINOR ROYALTY

Dead art doesn't interest me.
I'd rather watch a black cat
   dance in the sun.
Her sides are silver, her eyes
   gleam gold
her face is Egypt mapped
Base-born Siamese, I love you
200 years ago
they'd have burnt us both.

Our cats are well and thriving on their *Vegecat*. Purrie, alas, never recovered from her partial blindness [incurred prior to *Vegecat*]. But she still enjoys life. We have a large, sheltered back yard with a six foot fence. On sunny, winter days, she like to sit out on the grass and listen to the birds singing "musical meals." I have told the children that if they can imagine how they would feel if they saw chocolate and rice puddings fly about emitting sound, then they will know how cats feel about birds!

The good news is the excellent effect *Vegecat* had on Melaney, our beautiful Siamese. Mel is 10 years old, and was acting her age. But after just two or three weeks of *Vegecat* supplement, she was literally racing around and behaving as playfully as a kitten. It was wonderful to see her return to her old self. Ossie, our chinchilla, also benefited.

...Did I ever tell you Melaney won two first prizes at the local cat show on her vegetarian diet? Alas, her prizes included a complimentary tin of horrible old Jellymeat!

Just before press deadline we sadly learned from a just arrived letter that Ann had recently suffered grievous losses:

I put off writing on this before because it is still a painful topic. Since Xmas we have been doubly bereaved — of our much loved three cats, only Ossie survives. ...Melaney was my elder boy Richard's cat, and Purrie belonged to the younger one, Ian. A strange thing that almost every cat we've had has met a violent end either through cars or dogs. Our property is well-fenced and gated, but as you would know, this is no deterrent to the normal cat.

Of the cats who have given me the privilege of their friendship, Melaney was my favorite. We had her for twelve years. No photo we took ever did her justice. She was at least half Siamese and had the proud grace of a princess. The lion is acknowledged king of the animals, and Mel knew she was his tiny domesticated cousin, but his cousin nonetheless.

We first noticed the airs when she was a kitten. At the time I was fascinated by the hauteur of this nondescript black kitten. It wasn't till she was half grown that her pedigree became apparent. That is, to us — Melaney herself always knew she was class!

We acquired her a few months after my husband's death. The boys were playing outside a neighbor's when the latter emerged to return their cat to the RSPCA. She had committed the "crime" of having babies.

"He kids, wanna kitten?"

The boys were delighted. I was appalled. We were strict lacto-vegetarians. Cats are carnivores. How on earth would we feed it? The kitten must go back to wherever it came from.

The boys howled, clambered and protested. Finally I gave in. No doubt the cat would move on when it found our vegetarianism was inflexible. Besides, it was hard not to feel unwilling sympathy for the tiny scrap sitting on the hearthrug. She was literally trembling with fear.

...Having acquired one kitten, we had to get another because Melaney missed her mum and siblings. So Eleanor joined our family.

At first I fed the cats on millet porridge (having read somewhere that millet is virtually a complete food) plus milk. Over time we altered the millet to the mixed cereals porridge recipe I gave you in an earlier letter. As well, the cats had powdered milk biscuits to crunch for their teeth (they loved these) and were each dosed daily with four garlic oil capsules. These kept them in good health. They never needed worming and seldom had to see the vet except after accidents.

Three years ago I substituted propalis capsules for reasons of economy, but still think the garlic was best.

Despite the fact only vegetarian food is available from us, no cat has ever deserted us for a home where the menu is more to their taste. People who dislike cats give as one reason that cats are incapable of giving genuine affection to the humans whose homes they share. This hasn't been our experience. My elder son says whenever he felt misunderstood by the rest of us, Melaney was particularly loving towards him, purring and rubbing her head against his hand. On cold nights she liked to sleep *in* his bed, burrowing down to his feet. When she decided it was time he got up in the morning she would waken him by gently scratching his soles!

Sometimes, late at night, I go down to the post office or corner store. Though I never called her, Mellie would be there at the click of the gate — a small dark shadow racing ahead and to the side. She never accompanied me the full distance, but would wait at the street corner. Returning, I'd hear that penetrating Siamese Eeeee-owWWW that said emphatically as words: "Took long enough, didn't you? You should know better than to make ME wait and worry! But I'll forgive you."

Oddly enough, it was only after sunset that she escorted me on these walks. Perhaps she sensed it wasn't wise for human females to walk alone.

A few months before her death, I took her to the vet. She had had a lump under her stomach for some time. I'd managed to save enough for her to have an operation if she needed one. Mercifully, the vet thought an operation would pose more risk to her than letting the lump be. When told she was 12 years old he seemed surprised. She was very healthy for her age, he said. We could expect to have her with us another five or six years.

We had noticed Mellie had become almost jealous of we humans in some ways, especially in the food line. It was as if she was accusing: "You give yourselves more interesting food than you do me. It's not fair. I want to share!" We put tea scraps out for the cats. But Mel had decided she wanted to eat with us. Usually she sat on the floor by Richard's chair. But if we were having something she really liked she might jump on the table and snatch it off his fork! (I must confess we were amused by her cheek, and discipline attempts ranged to halfhearted to non-existent.) Meal times in our household are erratic but somehow Melaney usually knew when tea was ready. On the evening of December 9, 1991, her time was out. We had just finished eating when she walked in. The boys chuckled at her affronted air.

"You're too late, Mellie darling," I told her, and carried on talking to the boys. Five minutes later, relenting, I searched in the fridge for her favorite processed cheese. But she was no longer in the kitchen. Nor did she come when called.

She didn't sleep on Richard's bed that night either. He missed her company, but wasn't concerned. In summer she occasionally stayed out all night. I didn't worry either till after 8 o'clock. It was unlike her to miss breakfast.

"Have a look for her, Rich, something might've happened," not really believing my own words.

Five minutes later he was back, his face white beneath its tan, "Mum, don't cry, but Mellie's — dead..."

Reconstructing, we learnt a car had swooped into the joint drive we share with a neighbor, probably at illegal speed — too fast for a crossing animal dazzled by the headlights swinging round the corner. The heartbreaking irony is that Melaney had an intelligent respect for moving cars.

Our one consolation is believing the cowardly (he never fronted to apologize) killer who robbed our beloved Mellie of a cherished old age, takes on himself all bad karma due in those years. And believing too, that our pet who went against her carnivore's nature out of love for her people will surely be granted human birth in her next life.

...P.S. (two days later) Before posting this, perhaps should mention that after a six-month campaign on his part, we have been adopted as members of his extended family by a neighboring cat. Grayson (as we call him) is an enormous gray tom. His owners put him outside winter nights because they have a baby. Though we don't have snow, winters here are still chilly.

It didn't take Grayson long to discover our cat door is left permanently ajar for Ossie's benefit. And that chairs and laps by the woodburner are warmer than sleeping under our house.

But he is too big to easily squeeze through the cat door. Thumps and clatterings from the laundry always signal Grayson is gamely fighting his way in, one massive shoulder at a time —luckily the door is sturdy!

The endearing thing about him is the way he loves vegetarian cat food. What are you to do with a cat that literally squeaks with joy at the prospect of "Vegecatised" cat porridge? — then bolts every mouthful, purring loudly?

His owners complain Grayson has lost interest in his meat. So I've stopped giving him the vegetarian breakfast he politely requests after a night at our place. Instead he's firmly but regretfully sent home out of fairness to his owners. I've also stopped giving him tea. Nothing daunted, he now turns up for a vegetarian morning tea and supper!

It does look as if he wants to move in with us, but ethics aside (he *does* have a good home) we couldn't afford to care properly for such a big animal.

But he's a very welcome visitor.

Carolyn Gossman, an early pioneer from Pennsylvania, sent the following picture and letter and mentioned that her cat was small. It's a good thing that we aren't entering fat baby contests! Early research stated erroneously that food putting weight on fastest was the best. That's simply not true. Scientists now believe that slower (but sound) growth leads to a longer life.

Here is my cat, Alyosha. She's two years old now and has been a *"Vegecat"* since seven and one-half weeks of age. I started her on your recipes immediately when I got her (by the way, I found her on the streets of Philadelphia — so she's lucked out!). It wasn't hard getting her on the food or the supplements. Now she'll eat ANYTHING! I never knew a

ALYOSHA

cat would ever like vegetables! Her favorite treats are carrots (made any way), string beans, peas, French fries, potato chips (we use these to bring her out of her hiding place — she just has to hear the bag rustle and she comes running) and bread.

I've tried several of the recipes and have found that she likes the vegan oatmeal recipe the best. I mix vegetables in with it also.

I've noticed several things that are different about her. She's smaller than most cats. She doesn't shed as much as other cats and her coat is shinier and softer. She also has a wider range of food tastes, which I think is healthier than the diet most cats are one.

Sometimes her love of a food gets her into trouble. Like when she drags melon rinds out of the garbage and eats them — then lies around all day looking green at the gills. She has also eaten pastries and breads out of the wrappers.

Whenever people hear that she's vegetarian they don't believe it. When my parents confirm it, then people always comment, "Well, that sounds cruel." I then point out that since she's perfectly healthy, I don't see what's cruel about it. Alyosha likes all the different foods she eats — and likes to taste different foods; usually if I'm eating it, she wants it.

Any vegetarian who's not sure about putting their cat(s) on a vegetarian diet shouldn't worry. My cat grew up on a veggie diet and she turned out to be perfectly healthy — and then some. Making her meals are as easy for me as opening a can is for people who feed there animals commercial junk pet food. I take every opportunity to tell people about her diet and how well she's doing, and how much more cheaper it is.

Ralph and Vona Marengo in Massachusetts sent us two profiles, one on a part blue Persian, and one on a black poodle:

SHANTI & ZARABETH

Late afternoon, on the day after Thanksgiving 1984, my husband, Ralph, came in and said with a mischievous look, "I almost brought you a present!" Knowing he'd been to the Animal Rescue League to take pet food coupons to them, I sighed: "Must have been a cat..." My sweet, elderly lady cat, Babet, had died in 1982 at the age of 18 years and ten months, and I vowed NO MORE CATS. The pain is just too great.

SHANTI

Ralph proceeded to tell me about the adorable 8-month-old part blue Persian with golden eyes, who looked right at him and "Meow," and would I like to go see him? Obviously, that's what I did, because I'm a longtime sucker for cats!

Holding that skinny ball of fluff in my arms, I explained to him that he'd have to eat vegetarian food or we'd have to bring him back to the shelter! He ate the first thing I offered to him — some baked potato! To this day he thinks baked potato is ambrosia! He'll climb up on the side of my leg and bat me with his enormous double paws if I'm fixing potatoes, or he'll climb into my lap at the dinner table.

Thinking I could surely feed him well, I came up with my own vegetarian recipes for feeding him — actually it was very much like one of the recipes that come with *Vegecat*, minus the oil mix and *Vegecat*.

Unfortunately, after three years, we began to notice some rather strange behavior. Shanti was running into things and he couldn't find the stairs when I brought him in on his leash (he's tethered in a spacious yard with a six foot fence, a tree he can climb about five feet into, and plenty of shade and water). I was getting very worried.

I went looking through back issues of *Vegetarian Times* magazine for something I'd seen about a vegetarian cat supplement. When I found it, Ralph called Harbingers to talk to Lynn and James. But they weren't too encouraging. They thought their supplement could arrest his problem, but not improve it. We ordered their book *Dogs & Cats Go Vegetarian* and some *Vegecat*. As soon as the supplement arrived, Shanti began to be nourished.

In about a month's time we began to notice a marked difference in Shanti! He seemed to be more able to negotiate obstacles! As time passed, his eyes improved greatly. We are so pleased that he no longer tries to go through and/or up the wall instead of the patio stairs. He still had trouble judging distance in height, so we made him a box about a foot high as a step to get up to his food on a counter in the sun room. He now lands safely on the counter. Before *Vegecat*, he was missing, and falling off or crashing into the counter nearly every time. (In case anyone wonders why we don't just feed him on the floor, Zarabeth, the dog, would have his dinner and hers too!) Sometimes he still bumps into things, but he can spot a chipmunk on the fence 25 feet away! (We think he's a bit farsighted.)

The change in Shanti's eyesight is amazing — I think without *Vegecat* he'd be blind, and that just wouldn't be fair! Shanti says, "Thank you!"

Zarabeth (named after one of the two women Star Trek's Spock kissed) came into our lives 15 years ago. Our 11-year-old poodle had died, and Ralph wanted another dog.

I wasn't too excited about the idea as I'm a real cat person. A friend called to tell us about a black poodle who was to be executed in three days at the Millbury Pound; needless to say, this shaggy, mangy, scabby mutt came home with us!

She needed salve for the mangy eye, two baths a week for the scabby belly, and ... well, nothing would help the scuzzy fur! She won a place in our hearts with her wonderful personality, though.

About 10 years ago she developed an anal abscess and the

ZARABETH

vet wanted to operate but told us Zab would probably lose control of her bowels. We contacted Jo Willard, a Natural Hygienist in Connecticut and asked her advice. She suggested a fast, hot and cold compresses followed by a vegetarian diet, all of which we did. Zab recovered, and became a vegetarian!

Unfortunately, she got quite chubby and with age she developed cataracts and arthritis. I figure she had eaten the stuff from the supermarkets long enough to cause problems later in life.

Last summer she broke a leg and was confined to bed for three months. It became a flying carpet as we carried her from room to room on it so she could be with us! It was also her bathroom, as she couldn't stand or walk — we washed a ton of towels!

The vet said that at 15 years she probably never would heal and I just couldn't face that! I sent for *Vegedog* to make sure she was getting the best nutrition possible.

I made up the *Vegedog* supplemented food and faithfully gave her that and the next check up (about three weeks later) her old bone had healed! She also lost about eight pounds that makes us very happy. She's also kept it off!

Her arthritis was getting worse and she had lost all the fur off her tail, lower back and back of legs and was losing more on her shoulders. Some mornings she seemed to be in great pain — she'd cry out as she lifted herself to a standing position. We took her to another vet (the broken leg vet experience was not good) and he said she had a hormone deficiency probably caused by a tumor on the adrenals and arthritis and she'd need some "pills" (one was an anti-inflammatory and one was a pain killer). She now gets half of a buffered aspirin a.m. and p.m. and the steroid once a week. She seems pain-free and is quite frisky for a 16-year-old "lady."

The most interesting thing is her hair is growing back! She probably won't get it all back, but it's a big improvement! No longer does she have a "sausage tail" and a "baboon bottom." We attribute this to the *Vegedog* supplement.

FLETCHER

Although I have four vegan cats that I adore equally, I feel most inclined to write you about my 2-year-old Russian Blue, Fletcher. All of my cats were strays, coming from a variety of backgrounds, but Fletcher's past is, doubtless, the most depressing and pathetic.

My boyfriend, Ben, found Fletcher a year ago on a subway in New York City. He lived in a small crate that was caked with filth. Two homeless boys, barely able to care for themselves, fed him what they could from time to time. When Ben bought Fletcher off of them for 20 dollars, it did not look like he was going to make it. He was obviously severely dehydrated and malnourished. He had great difficulty walking; it seemed that the muscles in his legs had atrophied from living in the crate. His head was enormous for his small, bloated body and his fur was dry and matted. He was infested with fleas, mites, intestinal worms, and ringworm was spreading on various parts of his body.

FLETCHER

He also had severe behavioral problems, as would be expected, and had a tendency to attack rather viciously when something scared him.

He was such a mess it was overwhelming, but I was afraid that a veterinarian would insist on putting him to sleep. So we decided to do our best on our own.

Knowing where to begin was the most difficult part. We bathed him, cleaned out his ears, and used various herbs to treat the mites and ringworm (tea tree oil is excellent for getting rid of fungus). We treated him very specially and with great care so as not to frighten him. We warned visitors not to pet him (we lived in a very tiny one-bedroom and couldn't really isolate him), but not many people wanted to visit us; everyone thought we were crazy!

Only a few months earlier I had begun the transition to feeding my two other cats a vegetarian diet. So Fletcher was introduced to my cats' favorite food at the time — ground chickpeas and brown rice mixed with veggies, oil, tamari, *Vegecat*, and tons of nutritional yeast. I also encouraged him to drink a lot; he especially loved soy milk (it's still his favorite today), and to eat liquid vitamin E to help his skin heal.

Needless to say, he was by far the easiest convert to a vegetarian diet (I've converted four other cats to date). He still eats his food with gusto and maintains a perfect body weight.

Two months after we took Fletcher off the subway, we were moving to San Francisco. In order to take him on the plane, we had to get him a health certificate.

We took him to a holistic veterinarian. Upon examining Fletcher, the vet commented on what a beautiful and healthy cat he was and what a wonderful disposition he had. I laughed as I told him the condition we found him in only two months earlier. The vet was incredulous.

He was also interested in the natural treatments I used. I mentioned the various herbs and vitamins. But I also told him that I felt strongly that the healthy, vegetarian diet greatly contributed to Fletcher's quick recovery.

So I would like to thank you for the tremendous efforts you made to come up with a healthy and ethical diet for our animal companions. As an ethical vegetarian, supporting the slaughterhouse by purchasing pet food was always a dilemma for me. Discovering your product was a lifesaver, literally!

Jennifer Friedman — Oregon

Gwyn Watson wrote from Canada about two of her companion animals, Janus and Layla, enjoying a new lease on life:

JANUS

My two labs and six cats have been on *Vegedog* and *Vegecat* for about six months now.

I have a golden lab named Janus who is nine years old. He has had arthritis for the past four or five years. Over this time he deteriorated to the point where he could hardly get up the basement stairs and was very stiff and in pain when standing after laying down for long periods. It has been at least three years since he could jump into the back of our pickup. We either lift him in or carry stairs with us.

Since being on this diet, Janus has lost over 20 pounds, is now running, and has even jumped into the back of the pickup without assistance.

I make the Lentil-Sunflower recipe in large quantities (2 25-pound bags of lentils at a time) and then bake them into loaves and freeze them. That way I only have to make dog food once a month, or even less.

I was told one year ago by a vet that Janus wouldn't last more than a year. My present vet tells me Janus is in excellent shape.

My cat Layla had a chronic bladder infection. She was on medication from the vet three to four times per year for the last four years. When she was not on medication I managed to keep it under some control with liquid vitamin C. Any stressful situation (i.e., moving) caused a flare-up.

Since being on *Vegecat* she has not had any more trouble. I have not even been giving her the vitamin C.

LAYLA

We make the Oat-Soy recipe and add chopped up carrots and sprouts. I found that I had hardly any trouble talking them into this new diet, also.

...As a vegan it distressed me that I had to compromise my beliefs to feed my family in the past. I only wish I had read your book sooner. I could have saved Layla and Janus a lot of pain and suffering.

_____

DEGAN

This is Degan Cousens. He has been a vegan for four years. He is healthy, sleek, and energetic. People find it hard to believe that he's nine years old — he's so playful they think he's a very young dog!

I've been a vegan for about six years now. My reason for changing my diet was ethical, so it soon bothered me that my dog had to continue (I thought!) to support the slaughter-house industry. I didn't think I had a choice. However, through the PETA organization, I discovered that dogs could be vegetarians and that there was even a how-to book out on the subject. I was thrilled! Not knowing any-one else who shared my concern about the slaughterhouse industry, it was wonderful to discover other people felt as I did. I love the *Vegepet Gazette* because it makes me feel con-nected to others like myself.

Degan does great on the *Vegedog* diet. I also occasionally purchase prepared vegetarian dog food (both canned and dry) from Wow-Bow Distributors. I was happy to see that they are enclosing information about your book and products as well.

Lynne Cousens — Maine

_____

MOOKI & SNEAKER

We reproduced the first part of Arlette Liwer's story of her two kittens in the *Vegepet Gazette*, titling it, "Vegan Kittens in the Land of Flowers," because her family lives in the Netherlands.

Arlette wrote to the editor of *CATS* magazine after they printed that it was "absolutely unfeasible" for cats to be vegetarian. She corrected them, using her own two 8-month-old kittens as examples. Read their objections as well as her letter (which they printed) in Chapter 11. She wrote us:

For a year my husband Tom, and I, wanted kittens but I didn't want to get them before I understood how to feed them the vegetarian way.

I was very happy to find your book in Hawaii last summer. It was later recommended to my by Ihor Basko, a vegetarian veterinarian in Hawaii, and by the owners of a vegan restaurant in Maui. I read the book and ordered a year's supply of *Vegekit* and *Vegecat* before coming back to Holland and looking for our kittens.

We found our two little orange kittens, Mooki and Sneaker, five weeks ago. They were six weeks old. I would have preferred them to stay with their mother another week, but the woman who owns the mother was beginning to feed them and I didn't want them to get used to a meat diet. I did not want to tell the woman about our vegan plans in case she thought we were nuts and changed her mind about giving them to us. Vegetarians are rare in Holland. Vegans are extremely scarce. Vegan cats? I think that we have the only ones in the country!

I read the book again and really got into preparing all of their meals. The kittens love everything! We considered changing their names to "Potbelly" and "Snotnose" because they are always eating and always have some kasha, tofu, or avocado on the tip of their noses when they come and snuggle with us.

At the beginning I felt sorry for them because the *Vegekit* smelled so bad to me. But one night I discovered the instruction and recipe sheet in the bottom of the *Vegekit* container, and I started reading it in the kitchen (with some *Vegekit* still on it).

The kittens meowed for attention so I sat on the floor to read it. I couldn't believe my eyes when the kittens started going crazy over that paper. They were licking it and rolling on it for a long time. I couldn't stop laughing. That's when I stopped feeling sorry that they had to eat it.

Mooki and Sneaker are now almost three months old. They have never eaten eggs or cheese or milk or meat or fish. I'm not sure where or not it's because of their non-aggressive diets, but we've never seen such loving cuddly kittens in our lives. All of our visitors agree. The kittens are usually perched on our shoulders while we're walking around the house, or else they are playing around our feet or stomachs or whatever. Wherever we go, they come with us — in cars, visiting friends, shopping, or for walks. They are either in our coats or on our shoulders.

Tom and I have had other cats, but never cats like these. This is what everyone else tells us, too. I'm sure that the diet and the supplement have a lot to do with this!

So thank you for everything you've done — the research, the writing of the book, and the setting up of the business. Since I did not want to own an animal if it meant dealing with meat, you've made it possible for us to have kittens!

You mentioned a new [book] ...so I thought I'd tell you how much my cats love soy milk sprinkled with *Vegekit* and brewer's yeast. I give it to them every morning. I also cook their oatmeal in soy milk and it's their favorite meal.

It's really fantastic having cats who eat exactly what we eat. In the mornings, as I prepare my sandwiches for work, I always throw them some pieces of my brown bread, avocado, tofu, and alfalfa sprouts. ...This is so much more fun than opening smelly cans of cat food every day!

Recently we received an update on Mooki and Sneaker.

Mooki and Sneaker are nine months old now and doing great. Now that the weather is warm, they ride inside my jacket on the motorcycle, on our shoulders on the bikes, and along our bikes too. You have to see it to believe it. We live on a busy street so never let them out, but we take them to the park all the time and let them run around freely. They come back when we call them, and for emergencies, all we have to do is shake the yeast pill jar we always take along.

They're pretty good on leashes too, and this week, we are in the process of training them to use our regular toilet. But the best thing of all is how affectionate and loving they are to us and to each other.

Unfortunately they won't eat beans, no matter how we prepare them. What they love is crumbled up, defrosted tofu, just plain. And what they absolutely adore is tempeh. They try and reach the tempeh block every time we open the fridge. I'm experimenting mashing the tempeh with different cooked vegetables. They'll eat it with mashed potatoes. For treats I give them pieces of seaweed sheets. And at night they get a half cup of frozen peas, microwaved. Sneaker loves avocado and popcorn, and they both love corn chips.

When we went on vacation this summer, it was easy to give our friend a large frozen batch of breakfast mix, along with the frozen tofu and peas, and a few cartons of soy milk. If we get them toilet trained, it should be even easier to bring the cats to his house next time!

Cat Family Includes Mr. Bunny

Carol Clark wrote us from Illinois about her cats, and a white rabbit. A photograph of Socks with his bunny friend is on the next page, and Eclipse (another member of Carol's family) is on the last page of this chapter. We're sure Mr. Bunny appreciates the fact that his extended family doesn't eat animals!

I had to write to you to tell you about my situation at home and how much I appreciate the publication of your book. I never would have had the courage to try to feed my animals a vegetarian diet without your encouragement.

I have three cats, two dogs and my daughter found a white rabbit outside. The bunny sleeps in a dog bed and goes in the kitty litter and has the run of the basement. All of the animals get along, which is quite a miracle.

I tried many of the different recipes but the only one that my cats and dogs would eat is the one that I make using the oats and the textured vegetable protein. I like being able to mix up a big batch of it ahead of time because it goes fast enough as it is with all of the animals I have.

Socks & Mr. Bunny

The last time I had to take my animals to my vet, I showed him your book and told him that I was feeding them a vegetarian diet. He was not too impressed so I am buying an extra copy of your book so I can give it to him to read. I shall convert him yet! I told him not to form an opinion until he reads the entire book.

I started my pets on your diet in November of 1989. I wish I had thought or known of your book sooner.

Anyone who has had a dog suffering from allergies knows that helpless feeling of wanting to help, but how? It's been said, "Let your food be your medicine," and this is what Michael Buzel in Florida found to be true for his dog, Penny.

I adopted my first dog, Penny (collie/golden retriever mix) from the Florida Broward County Humane Society in 1987. She was four and one-half years old and suffered from multiple allergies that caused her to scratch constantly and gnaw at her backside. She kept losing a lot of hair and generally did not look very happy. I brought her to my first

PENNY

veterinarian who gave her cortisone pills that alleviated the problems. Unfortunately, cortisone causes other problems that are worse in the long run. When she stopped taking the pills, the problems recurred. I thought there has to be a better remedy than medication, so I found another veterinarian who suggested changing her diet. We eliminated all allergic foods (meat, chicken, fish, eggs, yeast, milk, etc.) using a commercial dry and canned dog food. It still contained lamb but Penny's condition dramatically improved.

After doing some volunteer work at the Humane Society, I became more interested in animal rights, subsequently becoming an ethical vegetarian/vegan. Penny was still eating her lamb and rice dog food, which made me unhappy, ethically, but I did not know how to feed her a well balanced meal using a vegetarian recipe.

Vegedog has assured the nutritional requirements of my dogs, enabling them to become vegetarians.

A friend told me about *Vegedog* and gave me a recipe for a vegetarian dog food (using a lentil base) and told me to supplement it with *Vegedog*.

Penny loves the food and I feel good about the food I'm feeding her. I cook the food every other Saturday morning (it takes approximately two hours start to finish) using two large stock pots. I make a lot because I recently adopted another dog in need of a home (golden retriever) who became a vegetarian when he became a member of my family. I never cooked in such large quantities before but the more I did it, the easier and less overwhelming it became. I freeze portions in large *Tupperware* containers and defrost as needed. I add *Vegedog* to their food at each meal, so I'm sure they are getting their nutritional requirements.

I wish more people would realize that they could try to help their companion animals with a change in diet like I did (in conjunction with a veterinarian's advice) which might stop the itching, scratch and hair loss as well as save huge amounts in vet bills.

Initially, Penny lost some weight when I changed her diet, but after adjusting her food portions, she is back to normal.

Her coat is shiny and she looks happy. She does not suffer from any allergic conditions any more. I also make treats for both dogs and give them carrots occasionally throughout the day for their teeth.

Again, if not for your food supplement and my friend telling me about your product, I'd still be facing a health and ethical dilemma every time I feed my "children."

ECLIPSE

Chapter 5

TEETH &

FOOD

I n the *Vegepet Gazette*, HOANA addressed a recurring question: "Does an animal need some hard food? I understand that chewing it will keep their teeth in better condition."

We responded to the inquirer's question by stating that there are conflicting opinions. The consensus is that dietary items can only help reduce tartar accumulation, and the bottom line is getting rid of tartar from time to time. Moist and canned foods make up 65 percent of the pet food market and their moisture content is about the same as *Vegecat* food. In commenting about dry pet foods, *Small Animal Clinical Nutrition* states,

> Their abrasive effect reduces (not prevents) accumulation
> of dental tartar, which promotes healthier gums and teeth.
> Most books on the care of dogs or cats do maintain that
> chewing crunchy food helps keep teeth free from tartar.

Anitra Frazier advises against dry cat food because it's a prime suspect in causing feline urologic syndrome (FUS). The justification for using kibble to clean teeth, she says, is "ridiculous":

Dry food does not clean the teeth, it never has and it never will. No one claims that, not even the dry food manufacturers. I have met numerous cats formerly on an all dry food diet with the worst tartar in the world.

Tartar

Although, phosphoric acid and corn syrup (in some pet foods) increasingly contribute to caries in the premolars of dogs and cats seen by veterinarian Michael Lemmon, tartar (dental calculus) on teeth causes most of the dental problems.

Tartar forms because oral bacteria on teeth trap food debris (plaque) along with the precipitation of calcium salts from saliva. Plaque forms mostly from grains and milk. Tarter looks like a yellowish-gray rim on the teeth, but in time accumulates to such an extent that it may become larger than the tooth itself. The gum swells away from the tooth, exposing roots, and bacteria get into the tooth socket. This is where massive infection, loosening of teeth, and abscesses form. Dr. Belfield says:

Teeth need to be kept clean in order to prevent the build-up of dental plaque (tartar). Accumulation of tartar initiates the gum tissue or creates a fertile bed for bacteria. I have actually seen animals with such a collection of tartar, bacterial infection, and pus in the oral cavity that they were systemically toxic and in mortal danger. By cleaning their teeth we were able to restore their health. Animals should have their teeth and gums checked by a veterinarian at least once a year and then cleaned if necessary.

Bones

Bones have a traditional reputation for keeping teeth clean. Dogs chew bones, and cats crunch on bony little creatures. Leon

Whitney recognizes this relationship between chewing bones and clean teeth in his book, *The Complete Book of Dog Care:*

> The quality of a dog's teeth is very little affected by the consistency of the food he eats. ...Whether a food is soft or hard is unimportant, so long as it contains a sufficient amount of the necessary elements. From the nutritional standpoint, hard foods may be either good or bad. The only special advantage that firm, resistant foods have is that they help tʳ clean the teeth...

> If every dog owner would give his pet a nice flat beef rib bone occasionally ...he would be sure that the dog, in crunching through the bone, would keep his teeth sparkling white. ...However, this should not be construed to mean that bones are essential for the development of sound teeth. Dogs fed meal-type (soft) foods reach old age with perfect teeth so long as the tartar is chipped off occasionally. A bone is merely a convenient toothbrush to clean off the tartar.

For dogs, one alternative to animal bones for helping keep teeth clean are nylon "bones" available in pet supply stores. For cats, Barry Bush, author of *Cat Care,* suggests using vinyl chew "toys," as a tartar preventive.

Vegetarian bones

> In *Keep Your Pet Healthy the Natural Way,* Pat Lazarus says,
> [Drs. Robert and Marty Goldstein] recommend giving your dog raw carrots (preferably organic), which are almost as much a challenge to chew up as are bones. Carrots will accomplish some of the ...teeth cleaning results provided by a bone. As for your cat, you could probably wait until doomsday before he would munch on a carrot, so the doctors Goldstein recommend you give him a firm biscuit made of whole grains.

Biscuits

Some veterinarians *do* promote whole grain treats for teeth and gums. Commercial vegetarian dog biscuits are available, and cats could have a limited amount of these. "People" crackers, such as the hard Swedish rye crackers in grocery stores may work as well. You could also make crackers or hard biscuits yourself. However, one school of thought theorizes that biscuits may actually increase gumline tartar since plaque forms from grains.

Rawhide chews

Rawhide chews are up to 10 times more effective in removing dental calculus than cereal biscuits, according to research conducted at the Harvard Medical School and published in the 1990 *Journal of the American Veterinary Medical Association.*

Each dog ate three rawhide strips or 10 dog biscuits daily besides dry dog food and water. The "treats" were given three times a day. After three weeks of treatment, rawhide removed 62.6 percent and biscuits removed 6.3 percent of the dental calculus from the maxillary fourth premolar. However they had little affect on other teeth, except for a gradual reduction of calculus on maxillary canines for dogs fed rawhide.

It is difficult to justify buying rawhide chews since they are slaughterhouse products. Rawhide chews do little more than biscuits to clean the teeth, and most teeth are untouched by either.

Do it yourself

Anitra Frazier advises examining cat teeth and gums every week. She goes into great detail:

Kneel on the floor with your knees apart and feet together behind you, and then back the cat in toward you. With you left hand, bring your thumb and forefinger under the cat's cheekbones and lift the head up, tilting it back as if to give a pill. With the right hand, lift the upper lips enough to peek at the gums and see if there's any tartar on the teeth. Then pull the lower lip down to check out the lower teeth. Also, insert the nail of your middle finger between the upper and lower front teeth and pull the lower jaw down so you can get a better look at the molars and the inside edge of the upper and lower teeth. On your first examination, become consciously aware of the difference in color between teeth and tartar.

In an article in *Cat Catalog*, Rebecca B. Marcus advises weekly cleanings: "use a toothbrush or moist, rough cloth wrapped around your finger; scrub the front teeth plus the gums."

David Taylor advises:

To prevent a build-up of tartar a cat's teeth must be kept clean. Many cats will agree to having their teeth cleaned once a week with a soft toothbrush, salt and water. If the cat resists, take it to the vet about once a year to have its teeth "descaled" under sedative or an anesthetic.

Barry Bush suggests using a small, soft child's toothbrush, dipped into tooth powder (other possibilities are baking soda powder or hydrogen peroxide). He says that cats don't like the froth and flavors of toothpaste.

Leon Whitney points out:

The removal of tartar is a job that can be done by any dog owner who is handy in such matters and not too squeamish. A special dental tartar scraper is all the equipment that is necessary. But your veterinarian usually will be able to remove all the tartar more quickly and with less discomfort to the owner and the pet. ...owners often delay taking their dogs to the veterinarian until there is as much as a quarter of an inch of tartar on the back teeth and the canines are heavily encrusted. By this time the dog's breath is usually vile. More than one pet owner has asked me to pull all his dog's teeth because they looked so horrible. In such cases I simply anesthetize the poor dog, clean every jot of tartar off, and when the master returns to claim his pet, show him an animal with a beautiful mouthful of teeth.

Links to vital organs

Veterinarian Donna Semich, while acknowledging risks are unavoidable when cleaning teeth using an anesthetic, warns of serious health problems if teeth are not cleaned. Even with teeth brushed daily by pet owners she believes a professional cleaning is necessary for getting under the gum line. This prevents periodontal disease — a source of infection to the rest of the body. She states: "Many pets suffer with heart, liver or kidney diseases that could have been prevented by proper and timely dental care."

Just this morning, a lady called about her 13-year-old dog (diagnosed with a faulty heart valve) who had difficulty breathing. She wondered what caused the heart condition. Sometimes it's congenital, but there's a good chance that it comes from chronic infection. Periodontal disease is a likely culprit.

Veterinarian dentists

Starting with just eight veterinarians in 1977, the American Veterinary Dental Society now has more than 1,000 members. Some veterinarians specialize in dentistry, performing root canals, oral surgery, putting on braces and crowning teeth.

Occasionally a dentist will have both a human and an animal dental practice, such as the one by Dr. T. Keith Grove, practicing in Vero Beach, Florida.

Only two veterinary colleges, at the University of Pennsylvania and the University of Illinois, employ dental instructors full time, and there are only four dental residency programs.

Dr. Colin Harvey, professor of veterinary surgery and dentistry at Penn and president of the American Veterinary Dental College, states, "every dog and cat merits a comfortable bite. You don't want to have to remove teeth when dogs and cats are old and at higher risk for anesthetics."

At least be aware

As caretakers of companion animals who share our living spaces, we have a duty to prevent sickness and prolong their years in as much comfort as possible. That means looking inside of their mouths occasionally and checking the status of their teeth. Examine them from time to time to see if they need cleaning (not all animal's teeth accumulate tartar). You can attempt cleaning them yourself, or let a veterinarian do it.

Go ahead and feed hard foods like crackers occasionally, but don't expect them to keep teeth clean. Once teeth are *really* clean, you'll know what to look for in the future.

Chapter 6

NUTRIENTS

A ny reputable company, wanting to develop food for cats or dogs, must start with reliable nutrient requirements. That is why HOANA started with research compiled by the National Research Council.

National Research Council

In 1863, the US government created the National Academy of Sciences (NAS). Chartered by NAS in 1916, the National Research Council (NRC) is the government's official advisor on science and technology, facilitating the interchange of data between government and industry.

Although in the private sector (non-profit), 85 percent of the operating expenses needed by NRC come from funding by the federal government. Without any laboratories of its own, it compiles and evaluates research done by others. Professionals serve on its committees without pay.

The Committee on Animal Nutrition is the one standing committee of the Board of Agriculture. Since 1942 it has developed nutrient requirement standards for at least fifteen specific species of animals.

The latest studies involving pets are: *Nutrient Requirements of Dogs* (1985) and *Nutrient Requirements of Cats* (1986) published by The National Academy Press. These two studies, modified by the latest research, provided data for formulating recipes using *Vegepet* supplements.

WATER

One-half of your companion animal's body consists of water. This makes it the most important nutrient. An animal survives if it loses all of its fat, one-half of its protein, but a ten percent loss of its total body water causes serious illness and another five percent loss causes death.

Prey eaten by cats and dogs during the last few hundreds of millions of years consisted of between 50-60 percent water. That water supplied much of their bodily needs for water. Today's pets usually are fed dry processed food containing salt.

One indicator of health is the proportion of water to total body mass. By eating fresh foods there is less chance body water gets replaced by excess minerals, therefore body flexibility persists into old age. Muscle tissues maintain elasticity in a healthy cellular environment.

Water suitable for cows and horses may be unfit for dogs and cats, so use water that you yourself would drink. Since ice cold water may cause intestinal cramps and diarrhea in an overheated animal, offer water at room temperature.

Bowls

Choose suitable receptacles with care. Cats like low sides so their whiskers don't touch. Glass and pottery (fired with lead free glaze) are easy to clean and look good. Feed stores sometimes stock heavy duty ones that stay in place, such as old-fashioned crock bowls for feeding rabbits, and they come in different sizes. Stainless steel is durable as well and relatively inexpensive. Galvanized containers may contain toxic amounts of zinc. Plastic containers are less durable since minute abrasions can catch germs and bacteria, unless kept scrumptiously clean.

ENERGY

The energy (calories) required per day varies, depending upon stage of life, ambient temperature and activity.

Energy Requirements

DESCRIPTION		TIMES RECIPE
1 HOUR LIGHT WORK		1.1
1 FULL DAY LIGHT WORK		1.4-1.5
1 FULL DAY HEAVY WORK (sled dog)		2-4
INACTIVITY		.8
GESTATION	(first 6 weeks)	1
	(last 3 weeks	1.1-1.3
PEAK LACTATION	2-4	
GROWTH	to 3 months	2
	3-6 months	1.6
	6-12 months	1.2
	3-9 months(giant dogs)	1.6
	9-24 months (giant dogs)	1.2
COLD	wind-chill factor 47°	1.25
	subfreezing wind-chill	1.75
HEAT	tropical climates	up to 2.5
DISEASE		varies

The above chart (extracted from *Small Animal Clinical Nutrition)* calculates daily food requirements. By multiplying daily portions by the indicated "Times Recipe" figures on the right, an approximation of how much food per day is required may be determined. However this isn't really necessary since animals fed natural diets eat for caloric needs and stop. Just make up substantial enough portions to adequately feed your animal for however many days you desire.

Donald Collins writes in his fascinating style:

The dog is a living creature. It lives because it burns — not in one great big fire, but in 100-million tiny fires throughout its body. If these fires go out, the dog dies.

The tiny fires burn in the cells of the dog's body. Except for a flame, the fires are similar in many ways to those burning in a furnace or in a fireplace. They both require fuel, they both require oxygen, and they both convert the fuel into heat and energy.

CARBOHYDRATES

Carbohydrates make up about three-fourths of the plant world, on which animal life depends. The word comes from its composition of carbon, hydrogen, and oxygen. All carbohydrates contain a ratio of two parts hydrogen to one part oxygen, just as in water. Green plants store the sun's energy as carbohydrates, either as starch, sugar, or both.

Carbohydrates are not a dietary essential, yet they supply energy and affect gastrointestinal functions. Most foods contain soluble or insoluble carbohydrates.

Commercial diets use wheat, corn, barley, and other seeds and grains as inexpensive sources of dietary energy. By using carbohydrates for energy, animals are spared using dietary protein, however excess carbohydrate intake results in obesity.

Digestibility of cooked or sprouted soluble carbohydrate varies from about 73 to 94 percent. Consumption of insoluble carbohydrates (fiber) results in the easier passage of food through the intestinal tract, with a larger, softer stool.

PROTEINS

When my first child was born, people asked "where does he get his protein?" Now, nutritionists tell vegetarian parents that there is *nothing* in meat that makes it a superior amino acid source for people. Cats do, however, require a *beta*-amino acid called taurine, obtainable only from animal sources or by synthesis.

Protein makes up one-half a body's dry weight. All living cells contain proteins, extremely complex substances made up of many amino acids. Of the 22 alpha amino acids, 10 are considered essential. Every protein molecule contains nitrogen, constituting 15-19 percent of its weight.

In examining diets, one looks for individual amino acids since their balance is necessary for growth and maintenance. Appendix 2 contains the amino acid content (as well as quantitative protein) for typical cat and dog diets.

To the body needing building materials, it doesn't matter whether the amino acids come from pigs or peas. Individual building blocks of amino acids are identical in both.

Taurine

For most mammals, taurine is a nonessential sulfonic amino acid. The liver biosynthesizes taurine from the amino acids cysteine and methionine, in the presence of vitamin B6. Felines, however, preferentially produce the amino acid felinine (probably for a territorial marker), making dietary taurine essential for cats.

One of the liver's functions is producing bile. Bile salts break globules of fat into minute sizes, the same as dish detergents cut oil off of dirty dishes. After treatment by bile salts the now miniaturized fatty acids and other lipids can be absorbed from the intestinal tract.

Most mammals make bile salts from both taurine and glycine. If a shortage occurs of one, bile salts are readily synthesized from the other. Felines create bile salts exclusively from taurine, and considering their limited ability to synthesize it, a shortage is critical.

Cardiomyopathy

NRC's recommendation for taurine was 500mg per kg dry food until 1987, when Paul Pion and Quinton Rogers published their research indicating that this figure was not enough to prevent cardiomyopathy. Cats with this degenerative disease typically live only a few days to a few weeks after its diagnosis since heart muscles turn flabby, limiting its ability to pump blood. Autopsies show that about 3 percent of the estimated 62 million cats in the United States die of this disease. After considering the new evidence, the official recommendation for taurine changed to 800mg per kg dry food, a figure HOANA has always used in formulating *Vegecat* and *Vegekit* diets.

In August of 1987 the *Los Angeles Times* bannered, *"Thousands of Cat Deaths Traced to Pet Food Deficiency,"* and continued the article on a following page with *"CATS: Deadly Shortcoming in Food":*

> Tens of thousands of cats have been dying every year from a form of heart disease caused by a nutritional deficiency in some popular pet foods, scientists at the University of California, Davis said in a report being published today in *Science* magazine.
>
> Pet food companies became aware of the problem in March and have reformulated their products to correct the deficiency, according to the Pet Food Institute, a trade orga-

nization. Among them was Purina *Cat Chow*, the best selling brand of dry cat food.

The deficient substance is an amino acid called taurine, which regulates the entry of a small amount of calcium into heart tissues each time the heart beats, said pharmacologist Steven Schaffer of the University of South Alabama. The calcium triggers each heartbeat.

Cats and humans are among the few mammals whose bodies do not make taurine and therefore must obtain it in their diet. In humans, taurine deficiency is extremely rare because taurine is common in meat, fish and clam juice.

Humans, as with most mammals, *do* synthesize taurine in their livers. Stating that taurine deficiency is "extremely rare" because people consume animals, implying people need to eat animals, is just one *more* myth about vegetarians.

...He found that every cat that had dilated cardiomyopathy also had low taurine levels, a total of more than 50 so far. When he treated the cats with taurine supplements, "the cats began to have miraculous recoveries," he said. "Their hearts would become normal again."

Diseased cats were fed a variety of commercial diets, including Hill's *Science Diet c-d* and *Maintenance*, Purina *Cat Chow*, 9 Lives *Beef and Liver*, Carnation *Fancy Feast Beef and Liver*, and Blue Mountain *Kitty O's*.

Blindness and more

As early as 1963, atrophy of the rods and cones of aged cats was described. By 1975, a link with taurine deficiency was made. Typical feline central retinal degeneration in adult cats or older kittens causes only partial loss of vision except in advanced cases. Without a dietary source of taurine, cats exhibit evidence of retinal changes in as little as three months. These changes become extensive within six months, and total blindness make take two years to develop.

In addition, taurine deficiency causes reproductive problems, slow growth, neurologic abnormalities, thromboembolism, and immune dysfunction. No one would wish to put their cat at risk, but some vegetarians unknowingly did just that.

Sally inquired about *Vegecat*:

My cat is already blind and has been for two years. She is now four — has been vegetarian all along (since birth). She doesn't hunt on her own, I think, because she was the 'runt' of her litter. Any chance she will regain her eyesight??? with this product?

Caught in time, retinal lesions may be reversible. Jim and Janet wrote to us about Tiger. When we found out how much loss of sight had already occurred, we rushed them extra taurine, although careful not to get their hopes up. They later wrote us:

Thank you for the taurine you sent us for our cat Tiger. We noticed a big improvement in his eyes after only about five days. We finished it up about one month ago.

His eyes seem fine now. He runs again and plays, squints in the light and once again sits in windows. He can see cats across the street again and his eyes seem as sharp as before.

The only part of his vision that I notice is not as good is his vision at night. A few times he ran out the door at night and I noticed he kind of strains his head to see across the street. But we're so happy that he can see again!

Before he ate *Vegecat*, we always gave him a small amount of meat with his food, but now he doesn't eat meat at all. We switched him over to a little cheese or eggs mixed with his food. We found his tastes in food have completely changed. Sometimes, in the middle of the day, we give him a snack of papaya, banana, melon, or avocado. He loves them, but years ago he wouldn't touch such things!

In England, Lin switched her cats belatedly to *Vegecat* after trying a vegetarian diet without supplementation. She wrote:

Having unwittingly fed my two cats, Tuppence and Kelly, on an inadequate vegetarian diet for some years (causing blindness in both), words can't express my joy upon discovering *Vegecat*. Both cats are now thriving on their new diet and, with the exception of the recipes with rice and soy beans, have responded incredibly well. They're eating and enjoying their meals better than ever before, and already I can see an improvement in their health. Only time will tell if their sight will be restored. I live in hope. ...From the bottom of our hearts, thank you for *Vegecat*. It really is a dream come true.

Some time later, Lin wrote to *The Cat* magazine asking for their opinion of *Vegecat*. For their comments and our response see Chapter 11.

How taurine is synthesized

Some people quote out of date references that state taurine is obtainable only from animal sources (or trace amounts from plants). Now, and for many years, it has been more economical to obtain synthesized taurine.

For those with a technical mind, taurine's synthesis starts with the Haber-Bosch process. Using iron as a catalyst along with high-pressure and moderately high temperature, ammonia (NH_3) is synthesized from air. Ammonia's hydrogen atom is replaced with a hydroxyethyl radical by adding ethylene oxide. This mixture, separated by fractional distillation, results in ethanolamine. Further chemical reactions result in ethyleneimine that is converted into crude taurine. In solution, it passes through activated carbon several times for purification and is then dried. Taurine can also be synthesized by sodium sulfite sulfonation of ethylene chloride followed by ammonolysis with anhydrous ammonia or with aqueous ammonia and ammonium carbonate.

Arginine

Arginine is abundant in natural vegetable protein sources, although it is sometimes singled out as one reason to include animal products in pet food. For examaple, Joan Harper, writing in *Feed the Kitty-Naturally,* says: "I do know that there are certain nutrients that cat cannot live without, and that these are found only in animal products. These are the amino acids arginine and taurine…"

There is certainly *no* lack of arginine in grains, seeds, or legumes. All of our recipes exceed the NRC recommendation for arginine by at least 30 percent without the need for supplemental arginine. Consumption of a meal devoid of arginine results in clinical signs of ammonia poisoning within one hour for a dog, and within three hours for a cat (vomiting, frothing at the mouth, muscle spasm and altered cellular metabolism).

MINERALS

Minerals maintain the acid-base balances, are components of tissues, regulate fluid transfer through cell walls, and are essential for many enzymes. They work with each other, therefore overall balance is important.

Calcium and phosphorus

Closely interrelated, calcium and phosphorus constitute the major minerals constituting bones and teeth. Calcium is also intimately involved in blood and nerve cells. Both cats and dogs have high requirements for these two minerals. Vegetarian foods are higher in phosphorus, but indiscriminately adding calcium can result in an imbalance. Optimum calcium to phosphorus ratios (by weight) are .9:1 to 1.1:1 for the cat and 1.2:1 to 1.4:1 for the dog.

Adding additional amounts of these two minerals to an already balanced food can result in lameness and pain, which is one reason we don't advise adding supplements to commercial diets.

Potassium

Deficiency of potassium results in poor growth, restlessness or
lethargy, muscular paralysis, lesions of the heart and kidney, and a
tendency to dehydration and locomotive problems. Adequate
amounts of potassium can be obtained from natural foods.

Sodium and Chlorine

Essential for metabolism, these two elements are easily supplied by some form of salt. Some advocate additional dietary salt
for feline urologic syndrome, inducing the cat to drink more water. However, salt is implicated in hypertension, therefore this has
its own risks.

Miso and soy sauce are preferred forms of salt. Use seven
times the salt measurement by volume if you decide to use these
gentler forms of salt. Imitation bacon bits supply salt and contribute greatly to palatability, especially for cats.

Magnesium

A deficiency of magnesium can be induced with over supplementation of calcium and phosphorus. Puppies manifest deficiency symptoms of anorexia, vomiting, decreased weight gain,
and hyperextension of the front legs.

Cats require magnesium as well as dogs, but for them the
problem is usually too much in the diet. Magnesium is a component of struvite crystals (magnesium ammonium phosphate)
which are the stones most responsible for feline urologic syndrome (FUS).

Iodine

Signs of iodine deficiency include thyroid hypertrophy, goiter,
apathy, timidity, hairlessness, abnormal calcium metabolism, fetal
reabsorption, and death. Excessive amounts are toxic.

Iron and Copper

Both iron and copper are essential to prevent anemia. Most iron is in the respiratory pigments. In case of dietary deficiency, iron sulfate is the preferred supplement form since it assimilates twice as efficiently as iron carbonate. Iron oxides have very little, if any, iron bioavailability. Iron is highly toxic in larger amounts.

Copper is required for normal iron metabolism as well as many other functions, such as the production of connective tissue. Clinical signs of copper deficiency include bone abnormalities and connective tissue lesions. Excess copper may damage the liver.

Zinc

Zinc in trace amounts is important for numerous bodily enzymes, bones, teeth, and skin. Signs of deficiency include skin lesions, emaciation, general debility, fatty changes in the liver, distended gallbladder, and kidney damage. Too much zinc causes a calcium or copper deficiency.

Selenium

Although toxic in large amounts, selenium deficiency manifests as muscular weakness, anorexia, depression, and coma. Used with vitamin E, it is efficacious in treating some diseases.

VITAMINS

Vitamins are regulatory molecules not used for energy or structural purposes. By controlling a wide variety of metabolic processes they function as police.

Divided into two groups based on whether they are water or fat soluble, vitamins from the latter group frequently cause hypervitaminosis due to the ease of do-it-yourself supplementation.

Vitamin A

Although essential for reproduction, sight, coat, and muscular integrity, too much fat soluble vitamin A results in anorexia, weight loss, decalcification, tenderness of extremities, degenerative lesions of the arteries and veins of the myocardium, as well as gall and urinary bladder problems.

As well as using preformed vitamin A (retinol), dogs can convert vitamin A from provitamin A carotenoids. Dark colored natural foods contain large amounts of beta-carotene, having the highest vitamin A activity. Carotenes are active only after being converted into retinol during, or subsequent to, absorption through the intestinal wall. Carotenes are not toxic, although a harmless yellow coloration of the skin occurs in large doses.

Cats cannot use beta-carotene since they are unable to convert it to retinol, which occurs in the intestinal mucosa in other species. Therefore cats must be provided with a preformed source of vitamin A. Natural preformed vitamin A is available only from animal products in which the animal has metabolized the carotene of its food into vitamin A, concentrating it in certain of its tissues, primarily the liver.

Fish liver oils supplied the drug trade with vitamin A until 1941 when war orders banned fishing vessels from the Pacific, and chemists began synthesizing it for the drug trade.

Synthesis of vitamin A

For those with a technical background, the following describes the synthesis of vitamin A (using no animal products).

Acetone, employed as the starting material, is prepared by one of four ways:(1) dry distillation of calcium acetate; (2) catalytic decomposition of glacial acetic acid; (3) fermentation of starch, or (4) the dehydrogenation of isopropyl alcohol.

An essential product in the perfume industry, b-ionone (synthesized from acetone) is lengthened by one carbon atom by glycidic ester synthesis followed by alkali treatment to give the a, b-unsaturated b-C14 aldehyde. This is condensed in a Grignard reaction with cis-3-methylpent-2-en-4-yn-1-ol, obtained by the addition of methyl vinyl ketone and acetylene followed by allylic rearrangement and factional distillation. The crystalline C20 diol obtained in the Grignard reaction is partially hydrogenated at the triple bond, then acetylated, and finally dehydrated via unstable halogeno compounds to give under rearrangement the crystalline all-trans-vitamin A acetate. Vitamin A palmitate is manufactured by transesterification of vitamin A acetate by means of methyl palmitate.

By 1966, production of synthetic vitamin A totaled over 830 *tons* in the USA.

Vitamin D

Known as the sunshine vitamin since sunshine is one of its sources to the body, vitamin D is technically a hormone. If insufficient amounts are produced in the body it must be provided in the diet, in which case it is a vitamin.

All animals with bony skeletons require vitamin D since it facilitates absorption and utilization of calcium and phosphorus. Vitamin D deficiency results in rickets. After growth, the requirement for vitamin D is minimal.

Vitamin D exists in two forms. Vitamin D3 (cholecalciferol) formed only within animal bodies, is sometimes called "D-Activated Animal Sterol," and obtained from the wool of (usually slaughtered) sheep. Vitamin D2 (ergocalciferol), a non-animal derived form used in *Vegepet* products, is obtained by exposing yeast to ultraviolet light. Both forms are equally effective.

Synthesis of vitamin D2

Dried nutritional yeast contains approximately .5-1 percent ergosterol. When irradiated in liquid form with ultraviolet light it changes to vitamin D2 by cleavage of one carbon-to-carbon bond in the ergosterol steroid nucleus.

Vitamin E

Vitamin E, an essential nutrient for all higher animals, derives from vegetable oilseeds (mostly soy) or by synthesis. Research on the requirements for dogs and cats used the synthetic "dl" form. Bioavailability of natural vitamin E is higher in animals except for the rat, although the synthetic form is more often used therapeutically. An advantage to the synthetic, which may affect some pets having a range of allergies, is its hypo-allergenic affect.

Requirements for vitamin E vary according to dietary composition. Animals fed fish exhibit much higher requirements because high levels of unsaturated or rancid fats destroy vitamin E. A deficiency manifests as muscular dystrophy, heart lesions, and "yellow fat disease" (steatitis) may develop.

As an excellent antioxidant for preventing rancidity in oils, recommended usage is 100-300 parts per million. Add 400 IU per quart for just opened bottles of oil.

Vitamin C

In their long evolutionary path, cats and dogs relied upon the vitamin C stores of their prey. In houses and apartments they have little access to former sources and have to make do with their own limited production, as illustrated by the following chart. Because clinical signs of vitamin C deficiency are not evident if cats and dogs aren't supplied with a dietary source (their bodies do produce a little), the NRC doesn't consider it essential. Holistic veterinarians say that misses the point.

DAILY BIOSYNTHESIS OF VITAMIN C

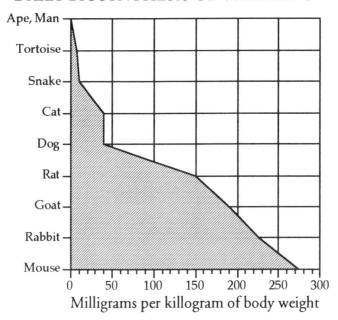

Milligrams per killogram of body weight

The most outspoken advocate for using vitamin C is Wendell Belfield. Along with Martin Zucker, he wrote two books that may be the best available on supplementation for companion animals: *How To Have A Healthier Dog,* and *The Very Healthy Cat Book.* People raise pets without benefit of vitamin C, and they apparently do fine, but as an "insurance policy" against sickness down the road, we recommend adding at least *some* vitamin C.

Belfield even recommends adding vitamin C before weaning. The following two charts gives his recommendations for cats as well as for different sizes of dogs. Hyphenated values mean that the dose gradually increases to the higher amount during that time period.

These doses are for *normal* conditions. Under stress or disease, raise the dosage gradually towards adult levels. If these amounts seem high to you, start low and observe the effects before going higher.

Vitamin C Dosage For Cats

Age	Milligrams
1-5 days	20
5-10 days	35
to weaning	65
First 6 mo.	250-500
Adult	500-750
Pregnancy	1000
Aged Cats	500-750

Vitamin C Dosage in Mg for Dogs

	Small	Medium	Large	Giant
1-5 days	20	35	65	65
5-10 days	35	65	100	100
to weaning	65	100	135	135
First 4 m.			500-1000	750-2000
First 6 m.	250	500		
4-18 m.			1000-3000	2000-6000
First 6 m.	250	500		
6-12 m.	250-500	500-1500		
Adult	500-1500	1500-3000	3000-6000	6000-7500
Pregnancy	1500	3000	6000	7500
Aged	250-750	750-1500	1500-3000	3000-4000

For very young animals vitamin C is available as pediatric drops. For older animals, use either tablets or convenient and (usually) less expensive powder, which easily mixes with food. Coating tablets with oil facilitates swallowing.

Diarrhea may mean either too large of a dose was given or the C was too acid. Sodium ascorbate is slightly alkaline and is more gentle. Both forms are just as effective. Read the section on FUS in Chapter 12 for more about vitamin C.

Mushroom gloom

Our sheltie, Kumari, gardened with us and learned to browse on her own. After I found that the mushrooms that cropped up every morning in our lawn were edible, I demonstrated to her how delicious they were. Every morning after that she grazed on the lawn, searching for the mysterious white plants that so accommodatingly popped up.

Visiting a fellow computer buff a few miles away, I discovered a magnificent spring amanita (listed as deadly poisonous). As a prank I took this orange and white "magic" mushroom and "planted" it in front of our door that evening as a planned surprise. A moment later, leading my wife to the door, I found Kumari's mouth chewing up the mushroom, relishing what she thought was a delicacy.

I had eaten amanitas years ago without ill effects and hoped this would have little effect on Kumari. Unfortunately, that night we found Kumari in trouble: trapped in a blind corner, disoriented and unable to see although her eyes seemed big as saucers.

Bringing her in, I gave her 2,000mg of vitamin C powder by putting it against her tongue and triggering a lapping reflex. Most of the night I sat with her, soothing and giving vitamin C. Towards dawn she relaxed and fell peacefully asleep. She recovered perfect health and you can be sure that I never brought those colorful mushrooms home again!

Thiamin (B1)

Beriberi, caused by a lack of thiamin, continues to be a human health problem in the Philippine and other parts of the world. Infants experiencing a rapid onset often die in just a few hours. Symptoms are cyanosis (too much carbon dioxide in the blood), tachycardia (fast heart beat), vomiting and convulsions. In adults the victim suffers swelling of the limbs which progress upwards until the heart chokes to death. Another form of beriberi manifests as gradual loss of body tissue along with nausea and confusion.

Cats and dogs also experience these symptoms if deficient in thiamin.

Riboflavin (B2)

Necessary for red blood cell formation, riboflavin also plays a role in protein metabolism. Some animals synthesize riboflavin, depending upon the type of carbohydrate in the diet.

Cats and dogs exhibit anorexia, loss of weight, cataracts, fatty livers, muscular weakness, and dermatitis if riboflavin is deficient.

Niacin

Many animal species can biosynthesize niacin from tryptophan, but cats produce virtually no niacin, and dogs do so poorly.

Deficiency manifests in weight loss, anorexia, weakness, and apathy. Thick saliva with a foul odor is characteristic, as well as ulceration of the upper palate. An association with respiratory disease is common, contributing to early death.

Pyridoxine (B6)

Vitamin B6 acts as a cofactor for a large number of enzymes involved in amino acid metabolism. A deficiency manifests as cardiac dilatation (enlargement of one or more cavities of the heart), congestion of various tissues, deterioration of the peripheral nerves, convulsive seizures, and irreversible kidney lesions.

Pantothenic Acid

Pantothenic acid demonstrates an involvement in the metabolism of food, synthesis of fatty acids, and other essential reactions. Deficiency results in emaciation and fatty metamorphosis of the liver.

Folic Acid

Necessary for growth, liver, and glands, folic acid also helps in the formation of red blood cells. A folacin deficiency results in weight loss, anemia, and a lowered white blood cell count.

Biotin

Widely distributed in natural foods, biotin is essential for fatty acid syntheses. It plays a part in other reactions in which carbon dioxide fixes into organic molecules.

A deficiency results in dried secretions around the eyes, nose, and mouth, as well as bloody diarrhea, anorexia and emaciation.

Avidin, a protein that binds biotin, is present in raw egg white. Some suggest not using raw egg whites for this reason, but if fed with egg yolks there is no risk since the yolks are so high in biotin. Cooking eggs lightly destroys both the avidin as well as a trypsin inhibitor that interferes with protein digestion.

Cobalamin (B12)

Vitamin B12 is present in all mammalian cells and is essential for their normal functioning. Since it is formed principally by bacteria, plants contain very little B12. A deficiency results in arrested growth and anemia.

Synthesis of vitamin B12

Commercial production of vitamin B12 uses the synthesizing ability of either bacteria (one-celled micro-organisms) or streptomycetes. The organism (most commonly propionibacterium freudenreicheii) grows in 10,000 to 50,000 gallon tanks on a medium of yeast extract, minerals, and sucrose or other carbohydrate for 72-120 hours after inoculation. Vitamin B12, contained almost entirely in the cells, is separated by centrifugation and then the final broth is dried.

The production of streptomycin and certain other antibiotics produces some vitamin B12 as a byproduct.

Choline

Choline is essential in cell membranes and lipoproteins involved in the transport of fat-soluble substances. It is also important in the brain and nerves. Although synthesized by the body, adequate choline requirements requires a dietary source.

Deficiency results in fatty infiltration of the liver as well as kidney disease.

ESSENTIAL FATTY ACIDS

All animals require certain polyunsaturated fatty acids. For dogs and cats these fatty acids stimulate growth and cure dermatitis characteristic of diets low in fat. Cats have a dietary requirement for arachidonic acid as well, which dogs synthesize (as do most other mammals) from linoleic acid, easily obtained from vegetable oils.

Linoleic acid

Linoleic acid, although a dietary essential, must be limited to cats fed a totally vegetarian diet. In cats, an abundance of linoleic acid competes with arachidonate, another dietary essential fatty acid for cats. Choose oils lowest in linoleic acid, such as (in order of preference) olive, high oleic safflower, canola, peanut, sunflower, and sesame.

Unsaturated fatty acids become rancid and lose their nutritional value if stored at warm temperatures or high humidity for long periods. An acrid taste warns of rancidity.

Arachidonate

Research in 1975 discovered that cats, unlike dogs and most other mammals, lack the desaturation enzyme in their liver that converts linoleic to the essential fatty acid, arachidonate. A dietary source for felines is therefore mandatory.

Arachidonate is crucial for the biosynthesis of some prostaglandins, fatty acid derivatives that have a variety of potent biological activities of a hormonal or regulatory nature. A deficiency of arachidonate results in mild mineralization of the kidneys, higher fat content of the liver, inflammatory skin lesions, and higher lymphocyte production. If the oil supplied in the diet has a relatively high level of linoleate (such as in safflower oil), the platelet count in whole blood can decrease by as much as one-half.

Bleeding

Mammals evolved a high blood pressure circulation system. In parallel with this, mechanisms to prevent bleeding (hemostatic) also evolved. Three components comprise this mechanism: blood clotting, aggregation (collecting together) of blood platelets, and contraction of blood vessels. If any one of these is defective, persistent bleeding may occur from slight injuries.

Blood platelets are nonnucleated cells, one third the size of red blood cells. They maintain the integrity of the vascular tree by sealing walls of injured vessels and contribute to coagulation. Cats lacking dietary arachidonate can experience longer bleeding from injuries because of delayed and weak platelet aggregation.

However, the most sensitive barometer of arachidonate deficiency is reproductive failure in female cats.

Arcane arachidonate

The search for a non-animal source of arachidonate led HOANA on a serpentine search. It's easy to come by, *if* you don't mind sacrificing animals for their livers. It was a long time before we discovered the aquamarine brick road leading to a non-animal source.

We called the chemist who had isolated ethyl-arachidonate for Ralston Purina. When we told him we wanted a non-animal source, he mentioned a study that indicated gamma-linolenic acid (GLA) might substitute for arachidonate. Then we talked with Dr. Marnie MacDonald, one of the researchers who had worked on the arachidonate question (along with Drs. Quinton Rogers and James Morris). She was kind enough to send us a copy of Theresa Frankel's 1980 Ph.D. thesis from the University of Cambridge (U.K.).

Frankel's research dwelt on whether GLA might substitute as a dietary source of arachidonate for cats. Her research found that many clinical signs of deficiency did improve, but were not entirely negated. For example, reproduction in GLA supplemented queens resulted in kittens with grossly abnormal brains.

A call to Dr. John Rivers just as he finished teaching a class at the London School of Hygiene and Tropical Medicine pointed us in the right direction. Rivers had co-authored, with Frankel, a paper on essential fatty acid deficiency in 1981, and seemed to be the next rung on the ladder of inquiry.

We recorded that conversation:

...There may be some obscure plant source of arachidonic acid and these other compounds. I don't know whether there's a plant source, but I should imagine if you look long and hard, you might find one. The plant source will probably be algae. Now, what you need to do is to talk to someone who's interested in fatty acid composition of food. I'm sure that algae will be a good source, the green scum that grows on the sea, and then see if you can get an acclaimed fatty acid biochemist to check it for you.

We then called Dr. Andrew Sinclair in Melbourne, since he had also worked with cats to study their conversion of GLA to arachidonate. He also pointed to the sea:

Now, some seaweeds have some of the uncommon fatty acids, although they wouldn't be very high in fat. There may be some seaweed products around. I know in the health food stores there's seaweed material available. Whether you could buy a seaweed meal, it'd be pretty pricey, I imagine. But the price for doing something that's different is often a high price, because you're doing something that's special.

Avocado branch

With renewed energy, we pored over the scientific literature, especially by Japanese marine scientists. In the meantime an amazing USDA reference popped up that stated avocados contained *substantial* arachidonic acid. Since we *loved* avocados, and avocado oil was readily available (however, expensive), we blissfully (howbeit briefly) thought our search was over.

To be absolutely certain (since this seemed such an unlikely source) we laboratory tested avocado oil. To our immense disappointment there was not a trace of the elusive arachidonate. We called the person at the US Department of Agriculture responsible for including the flawed data in *Composition of Foods: Vegetables and Vegetable Products*. He didn't express a bit of surprise at our finding, since he felt that they had published that particular bit of data hastily. Unfortunately, we couldn't bill him for our out of pocket laboratory expenses!

Dose with nodosum

Repeatedly, Robert Ackman's name kept cropping up on technical papers relating to seaweed lipids. HOANA called the Technical University of Nova Scotia. There we found a fellow "cat person," reminisced about the finer points of eating dulse ("real sea food"), and then caught him up to date on our research. He expressed such enthusiasm for our efforts that it seemed we'd finally found our "acclaimed fatty acid biochemist." He sent us many reprints of papers with which we weren't familiar, but all of the seaweeds seemed to be too low in fat and too high in iodine for our purposes. Finally we found it!

We submitted this likely candidate for laboratory analysis. The results, using a Perkin-Elmer 900 Series chromatograph, were even beyond expectations — a relatively concentrated source of arachidonate, low in iodine, not tinged with blood. The harvester of this particular *ascophyllum nodosum,* George Seaver, said that in his nine-years-experience "coats and skins always improve with the addition of this seaweed."

Lipid content varies depending upon where the seaweed is harvested. We always obtain ours from the same location, validating the analysis with which we were so happy. That is how we were able to meet the NRC recommendation for feline growth, which is .04 percent of the dietary energy coming from arachidonate.

CHAPTER 7

SHOPPING LIST

In formulating companion animal recipes, we tried to use commonly found ingredients. Most of these will already be familiar and probably be in your kitchen, except possibly for nutritional yeast, especially for those living outside of the United States.

OILS

For cats, use only (in order of preference): olive, high oleic (not regular) safflower, canola, peanut, sunflower, or sesame oils. Oils other than these contain high levels of linoleate that increase feline requirements for arachidonate, in short supply from plant sources. Dogs can use other oils as well, but these are good recommendations.

NUTRITIONAL YEAST

Nutritional yeast grows in purified cane and beet molasses solutions under controlled chemical, bacteriological, and sanitary conditions. It is not obtained as a by-product of any other process or manufacture.

Upon completion of the fermentation process, harvested yeast cells (*saccharomyces cerevisiae*) go through a wash and drying process. Pasteurization renders the yeast easily digestible and incapable of further fermentation.

Along with a protein content of between 50-52 percent, nutritional yeast supplies many vitamins, including pantothenic acid (70mcg/g), biotin (1.3mcg/g), choline (4mg/g), folic acid (5-13mcg/g), B12 (.001mcg/g), inositol (4.7mg/g), PABA (40mcg/g) and B6 (28mcg/g). As well, it is a rich source of minerals including trace (8 percent on a dry basis), binding them organically as enzymes and other growth factors.

In addition, it contains 10mg of glutathione per gram. Work being conducted at major research centers in the United States is investigating the apparent cancer fighting properties of this tripeptide that links the amino acids: glutamic acid, cysteine, and glycine.

Many agree that nutritional yeast is delicious, with a toasted, nutty, and cheesy flavor. Great on popcorn or salads, it's good to have around. Animals love it and we put it in every recipe. Coating chunks of food just before serving with a dusting of nutrition yeast increases palatability, especially for cats.

Don't confuse brewer's with nutritional yeast. They taste and look very differently. Nutritional yeast comes in flakes as well as powder and is a golden yellow in color, not tan like brewer's yeast. Many health conscious stores sell it in bulk.

If using flakes (instead of powder), double the volume (not weight) measurements for the yeast required in the recipes.

For awhile we thought that brewer's could substitute for nutritional yeast, since they were so similar in nutritional value. But it's not as desirable. Our dark cat, Ebony, has a little "trick." After we take the lid off a large bottle of brewer's yeast tablets, she reaches all the way to the bottom of the jar (as necessary) and picks up one or two tablets at a time with her delicate, curled up paw. She crunches them with obvious relish as Veggie wistfully looks on, trying to figure out how she does it.

Brewer's yeast tablets vary in palatability, as we found out when we ordered a new supply by mail. Ebony took the new ones out of the container but wouldn't eat them, and neither would Veggie. The tablets appeared lighter in color than the former, even though the container and labeling were the same as before.

Cat call

Remember Mooki and Sneaker from Chapter 4? Arlette and Tom love taking their cats with them on excursions. Independent, compared to dogs, cats sometimes (or is it always?) are slow to come when called. Many folks have told us about shaking a bag of corn or potato chips and their cats come running. Taking a bag of chips while out for a stroll in the park is inconvenient since protecting fragile chips can be a nuisance. Mookie and Sneaker come running when their caretakers shake the brewer's yeast tablet jar, just as sure as if they had heard a "cat whistle." Even though our cats don't like our current jar of yeast tablets, they still come around when they hear us opening vitamin bottles, and espcially if we shake them.

Getting back to their food, when we substituted brewer's yeast for nutritional yeast in their food, neither cat would eat it. I know people in other countries sometimes use brewer's yeast, since that is all they can find. But if given a choice, choose the tastiest.

The largest manufacturer in the United States for nutritional yeast is Universal Foods Corporation, selling it under the *Red Star* label.

WHEAT GLUTEN

Sold as "seitan" or in "burger" preparations such as Worthington's *Vegetarian Burger*, gluten is the protein portion of wheat. Properly prepared, cats (and dogs) love it for its meat-like texture and flavor. If you have an Oriental grocer nearby, try the Taiwan import "*Mun-Cha'i-Ya* (braised gluten)," which is less expensive than similar products. The label states:

Started in mid-10th century China, this delicacy was given the same taste and texture as roast duck, supposedly to keep vegetarians from swaying from their faith.

We always try to keep a couple of cans of wheat gluten in the cupboard. In a pinch or when traveling it's so easy opening a can and adding *Vegecat*.

If feeding cats this way regularly, add a small amount of olive oil and yeast along with the supplement. "*Mun-Cha'i-Ya*" is packed in safflower oil. Because of this, olive oil, as well as the usual yeast and *Vegecat* need to be added for complete nutrition. Instructions for making gluten (from whole wheat flour and water) at home are available in books such as *How to Make all the Meat You Eat Out of Wheat*, by Nina and Michael Shandler.

Although we haven't found them yet, "crab meat" and "caviar" from wheat gluten have been marketed. Wheat gluten has a glorious future since is it a basis for so many meat-like products and wheat is so easily available.

VEGETABLES

Cats and dogs usually like the addition of salad type foods. Finely chopped spinach, shredded carrot, and alfalfa or lentil sprouts are some possibilities. Our cats love frozen peas. We rinse them with hot water, plumping them up, and add them to their food. Sometimes they get thawed cauliflower and love it. They also enjoy baked or steamed squash and potatoes.

Add vegetables as enhancements, lending variety and palatability to regular recipes. Since veggies are low in protein, feed them in limited quantities since their bulk (and calories) could compete with protein foods necessary for good health.

Most cats and dogs seem to like grass, which aids the removal of hair balls, provides a source of enzymes, and is the subject of much speculation. If yours don't have access to a safe source, grow some indoors. Wheat, oats and sunflowers make for easy indoor gardens. Plant a new supply every two weeks. Once cats become fond of the blades, they nibble extensively.

LEGUMES & GRAINS

The healthiest legumes are sprouted. Amino acids increase (on a dry weight basis), synthesized from carbohydrates and fats. Research by the Indian Council of Medical Research showed that the growth promoting value and digestibility of garbanzo beans increases with germination. Francis Pottenger, Jr. found in his many years research with cats that, "Sprouted legumes and grains contribute enough first quality protein to be classed as complete."

Substitutions for Grains

Generally, grains can substitute for grains (i.e., rice or oats for wheat) and legumes for legumes (i.e., soy for garbanzo beans).

One cup cooked oats (7.8 oz. [222g] by weight) is equal to:

a- 1½ cups soaked bulgur (7.3 oz [206g] by weight)

b- 2½ slices of bread (2.2 oz [63g] by weight)

c- 1⅜ cups cooked rice (9.3 oz [265g] by weight)

d- Dry commercial cereals such as *GrapeNuts* or *Wheaties* (1.5 oz [42g] by weight)

Preparing Grains & Legumes

ITEM 1 cup dry weight	Add Water Cooking Time	Yield in Cups By Weight	
BULGUR	2 cups	2½	
4.9 oz (140g)	15-20 min.	16 oz.	454g
GARBANZOS	4 cups	2	
5.9 oz (167g)	3 hrs.	11.5 oz	326g
KIDNEY BEANS	3 cups	2	
6.5 oz (184g)	1½ hrs.	12.5 oz	354g
LENTILS	3 cups	2¼	
6.8 oz (192g)	45 min.	16 oz.	454g
OATS, Rolled	2 cups	2⅛	
2.9 oz (81g)	10-25 min.	17.5 oz	496g
RICE, Parboiled	1 cup	1¾	
6.5 oz (185g)	5 min.	11 oz	312g
SOY BEANS	4 cups	2	
6.6 oz (186g)	3+ hrs.	12 oz	340g

Substitutions for Legumes

One cup cooked soybeans weighs 200g but the dry weight is only 54g. One cup cooked garbanzos weighs 180g but the dry weight is 76g. This is why more cooked soybeans substitute for a lesser volume of garbanzos.

One cup cooked garbanzos (6.3 oz. or 180g by weight) is equal to:

a- 1 cup cooked red beans (7 oz or 200g by weight)

b- 1¼ cups cooked lentils (7.3 oz or 210g by weight)

c- 1 ⅜ cups cooked soybeans (9.8 oz or 275g by weight)

Soy can be in the form of "meat" analogs such as *Tuno,* a soy protein product from Worthington Foods that looks, smells, and tastes like tuna

d- 2 cups tofu (17.2 oz or 488g by weight)

e- ⅝ cup dry textured vegetable protein — *TVP* (2.8 oz or 80g by weight).

ENZYMES

In nature, dogs and cats consume warm prey filled with the elusive "life force." Many scientists believe our best substitutes for "live foods" are enzyme supplements.

Ideally, if your pet isn't getting adequate amounts of raw food, replace the enzymes lost in cooking. This saves the body the task of making digestive enzymes, taking energy away from manufacturing thousands of other enzymes, necessary for life.

A convenient powdered form, available in bulk is available from the National Enzyme Company, specializing in enzymes since 1932. We recommend their vegetarian *"Genuine N-ZIMES" Formula #1.* Nature's Way Products, Inc. recently introduced an entire line of vegetarian enzymes.

Cats and dogs enjoy fresh grass, perhaps partly because of the enzymes. For this reason alone it is good to occasionally add finely minced raw food to their food. Try sprouted lentils, olive oil, soy sauce, nutritional yeast and *Vegepet* supplement for delicious Lentil Italiano.

Chapter 8

FEEDING

FELINES

nstructions accompanying *Vegecat* supplement began with, "You are about to embark on an exciting journey. Your dream of vegetarian cats is about to come true. As a result of years of scientific research, and feeding trials in homes such as yours, *Vegecat* works. With no slaughterhouse products in your kitchen your cat (and the earth) will be healthier!"

'CAT'EGORIES

A) *Finicky Cats* eat only commercial cat food (and prey they may have caught). They are often timid and nervous. Easily distracted by the slightest disturbance, their eating patterns may include eating always from the same dish, in the same location, and away from other animals or people. Some, having been finger fed while ill, eat best forever afterwards when fed the same way.

B) *Non-finicky Cats* investigate a variety of different foods.

Value of novelty

Omnivorous species are subject to "food imprinting" or fixation of food habits. Dogs happily consume the same familiar diet day after day. Scientists believe this is because toxic edibles constitute the most serious challenge to survival of their young. By preferring familiar food, proved nutritionally safe over a considerable period, they are protected against poisoning.

Cats rarely encounter toxic food items as carnivores in the wild preying upon other living animals. Feeding trials prove that *unstressed* cats like an occasional change in diet, just for variety. Since they do enjoy change, their well known fixation to commercial foods is usually due to digest (see Appendix 1). It's such a powerful appetite stimulate that changing diets *can* be very challenging, requiring ingenuity and patience.

Sometimes cats so strongly refuse to eat that, in spite of good intentions, one wonders if plant foods are *totally* against their nature. According to David Taylor:

> ...all cats are carnivores... But this doesn't mean that cats don't like or need to eat some fruit or vegetable matter. Several wild cat species like to supplement their meat with the occasional fruit or vegetable tidbit. Lions and tigers, for example, often go straight for their victim's stomach after making a kill, devouring the soup of digesting vegetation as a starter...

Generations of pampered pets are creating a new kind of cat (especially with some purebreds). It has lost its natural eating reflexes and requires powerful appetite stimulants. This leads to more pampering, changing diets, etc., all adding to profits for pet food companies working with an entire arsenal of slaughterhouse products in their laboratories.

Making the change

First, give your cat a chance to eat the new food as a meal by itself. Many cats take to it right away, and if this is the case for you, one certainly wouldn't want to unnecessarily prolong an easy transition.

If rejected, mix a very small amount of the new food so well into the old food that your cat can't separate them. Gradually increase the one while decreasing the other.

David Taylor, writing in *You & Your Cat*, recommends:

When acting as a chef to a recently arrived "faddy" cat, the best way to introduce a new, healthier diet is gradually, adding the new foods one by one over several weeks.

Take as long as necessary for this transition. It may take many days, weeks, or even months. The goal is certainly attainable, but use your cat's time table, not yours.

Persevere

Linda Rooks wrote us from New Hampshire and told us that she didn't give up:

At first, my cats had a difficult time making the transition from a meat diet to a vegetarian diet, but with perseverance and commitment to making the change, my cats now love the vegetarian food I make for them.

They are healthy, slim, active, bright, and shiny. I have found they like especially a mixture of bulgar and lentils with some vegetables, cottage cheese, nutritional yeast, and oil. With the *Vegecat* supplement I don't have to worry that they are not getting everything they need and more on this diet.

If it seems you've reached a stalemate, with no further progress, then perhaps it's time to consider another tool, hunger.

Harbingers of a New Age

717 E. Missoula Ave., Troy MT 59935-9609 • USA

ORDER FORM PLEASE PRINT

Name _____

Address _____

City _____ State ____ ZIP _____

Ship to (if different) _____

_____

_____

Phone (home) _____ (work) _____

QTY	DESCRIPTION & SUPPLY *	EACH	TOTAL
	Small *Vegecat* 8 weeks	7.50	
	Medium *Vegecat* 4.5 months	15.00	
	Large *Vegecat* 9 months	27.00	
	Small *Vegekit* 1.5 months	7.00	
	Medium *Vegekit* 3.8 months	15.00	
	Large *Vegekit* 7.6 months	26.00	
	Small *Vegedog* 4 weeks	6.50	
	Medium *Vegedog* 2.1 months	13.50	
	Large *Vegedog* 4.2 months	24.00	
	N-Zimes powder 5 ounces	18.50	
	Vegepet Gazette 4 issues	12.00	
	Vegetarian Cats & Dogs (Peden)	13.95	
	Retailer information	Free	
	Information flyers	Free	

/93 **SAVE 10%** ↘	Sub-total	
Orders sub-totaling $96 or more, deduct 10%		
✈ For air delivery (USA), add 10%		
Add for shipping/handling (see next line)		4.00
For books only, shipping/handling is $1.50		
	TOTAL AMOUNT DUE	

*For a 10 lb (4.5kg) cat, 5 lb (2.2kg) kitten, or 44# (20kg) dog

Check ☐ # _____ MO ☐ COD($4.75 fee) ☐ VISA/MasterCard ☐

📞 Order: 800 88-HOANA Support: 406 295-4944

Signature _____ Expiration date _____

Guarantee: If not satisfied, return product(s) within 14 days for refund. VISA MasterCard

Hunger, the best sauce

Some cats, so surfeited with favored food, see no reason for eating something new and unwanted. Just like some people with pampered and catered taste buds, they never experience true hunger.

If this describes your situation, cut down the *size* of their meals (*not* the number). Feed them not quite enough each meal to satisfy their appetite. After a week or two of gradually diminishing meals, real appetite is going to return and the odds for a successful dietary change go up. Warning: in the face of persistent pleading from a "manipulator," caretakers need self-control. Deborah Edwards said in a recent issue of *Cat Fancy:*

...treatment is often more difficult on the owner than it is on the cat. The owner must learn to ignore the cat's pleading glances and plaintive meows.

This *doesn't* mean starvation. As Doris Bryant stated in *Pet Cats,* "It is cruel, and rarely successful." A short fast won't hurt, but don't let this dietary transition become a "battle of wills," with your cat the loser. Conflicts such as these only produce stress, and the more stress cats endure the more they insist upon their *familiar* foods.

How quickly your cat goes totally vegetarian has no bearing upon either you or your the cat. What's important is the direction you face, not the spot upon which you stand. Many influences, some before you may have acquired your friend, determine the ease of transition.

What cats recognize as "food" may have little relationship to what is actually before them. For a cat not trained in hunting by his mother, a mouse scampering across the floor looks less like dinner and more like a plaything. Cats famiar with kibble may refuse moist food. In the case of vegetarian, home prepared meals, not only are tastes different, but so are the textures and smells as well.

Maybe your cat is so malnourished from lifeless commercial foods that he or she has no appetite for anything but those foods. In that case the gradual transition may be such a slow process that, in the words of Doris Bryant, "the race may not be won." Administering a low potency B complex vitamin as well as vitamins C and E may succeed in bringing healthy appetite back. Coaxing, by offering bits of food in one's fingers or placing tiny mounds before them, may also speed the transition. The blue-green algae, spirulina, sometimes proves irresistible for cats and abundantly supplies easily digestible nutrients.

Mono-diet handicap

Unfortunately, *The Healthy Cat and Dog Cook Book*, written by Joan Harper, emphasizes meat: "Buy a whole beef heart and slice it into steaks or have it ground by your butcher. The steaks are delicious, like very mild liver but meatier." However, she's right when she talks about the drawback of continually feeding just one kind of food:

Cats that are finicky about food can easily become addicted to one type of food and refuse all else for days, even weeks. In fact they will almost rather starve to death than eat a diet they dislike. As they were originally desert type creatures, their bodies are very efficient at recycling water and can survive with little food for some period of time. So it is much easier to keep feeding many different kinds of food from the start, than to cope with a cat that is hooked on one kind.

Easy transitions

Some people have absolutely no problems making this dietary transition. Perhaps you will be as fortunate.

Amazed at the ease with which her cats made the switch, Eileen Henry of Ohio wrote:

I have been vegetarian for twenty years, and for twenty years I have had nothing dead in my house. I was anxious about getting cats, since they are carnivores, but because my two Dobermans, who love cats, are healthy vegetarians, I decided to give it a try.

I was really surprised at how easy the transition was when I got my kitties, Tiger and Minx. They absolutely love their food. Even my dogs like it.

Thanks so much for helping me maintain my lifestyle. My kitty's stools don't stink, and they are very healthy and happy.

Toni Leet in California also had an easy time:

My animal family include a dog named Bo (eight years old) and five cats — Max, Molly, Cheetah, Tux and Chloe (ranging in age from one to seven years).

I was surprised and quite pleased at how smooth the transition has been from meat-based pet foods to *Vegecat* and *Vegedog* — not a finicky feline in the family! They all look, act and feel quite happy and healthy, especially Bo!

Easy as opening a can

Carolyn Gossman of Pennsylvania mentions a common change occurring as a result of kicking the commercial food habit (addiction). Cats broaden their tastes in food, becoming adventuresome to the enjoyment of their caretakers:

I received your book and have already read it. I am so thankful I saw the blurb in the *Animal's Agenda!* Until then I didn't know what I would do if I got a cat. Now, making her meals are as easy for me as opening a can is for people who feed their animals commercial junk pet food.

She's been on your diet(s) since she was six and one-half weeks old. She's very healthy, and just as spunky as any other cat and she's very quick. She also will try ANY food and eats just about anything (she *doesn't* eat any animal products of course). I take every opportunity to tell people about her diet and how well she's doing.

Cat-egories A, B, and C

Cats (like people) are sometimes flexible and sometimes stubborn, and with every shade between. Californian Jean Bayard, introducing the new food to her three cats, found one of them very set in her ways. Rather than giving up, Jean felt a measure of success by just gradually reducing the proportion of old food to new:

I decided I would not cook the cats' food unless absolutely necessary, so I used the Oat-Soy recipe. Leo, not very fussy since until recently he had Hard Times as a stray, took to it right away. Sattva, who's got to be the grumpiest cat alive, and who we thought would really give trouble on this, accepted it, but grudgingly. Lani, whose appetite is delicate at the best of times, wouldn't eat it at all.

We had the full gamut so we set to work on Lani. For two or three days she didn't eat anything. We waited and hoped and watched but she would not touch the new food. I thought maybe it tasted bad and ate some myself. It was delicious (of course everyone to his/her own taste). Anyway, then I thought maybe she'll take the new food if diluted with the old food, so I put some of her accustomed kibbles in with the new food. She wouldn't touch it. In my worry I actually ran after her with one of the kibbles out of the mixture and she wouldn't touch it either! Then I realized she must be going by smell. The kibble smelled like the new food, and she didn't realize it was food. It looked the same but I'm sure it didn't smell the same.

So I started at the other end. I gave her a helping of the old kibbles out of the bag, and yes, she would still eat them. Next, I gave her the old kibbles with water over them. She still ate them. Next meal I ground up the old kibbles in the blender and gave them to her with water. She ate them. The next time I gave her the ground-and-wetted kibbles with a little bit of new food mixed in with it, and she ate that. Then I knew I had her.

Since then, every meal she gets ground up old kibble mixed with new food, the whole thing watered down and of course I'm gradually reducing the ratio of kibble. My idea is that in the process of eating the kibble, she'll smell the new food and be eating it too, and so come to realize it is food. (When we first got Leo he wouldn't eat anything but bread; that was the only thing he seemed to recognize as food.)

So far, we're down to half and half, and it's going fine.

I will not give up on this because it felt so good to become a vegan and know I was no longer exploiting and hurting other beings, and I'm not about to break it as long as I can think of ANY way to maintain it. That's why I'm so grateful to you for making *Vegecat*.

Expand food horizons

Cats almost universally love cantaloupe, fresh corn on the cob, peas, cooked squash, etc. Foods that you especially like, share with them. Let them get accustomed to new flavors and taste sensations. Experiment

Californian Steve Victor, author of the entertaining, *Light-hearted Vegetarian Gourmet Cookbook*, corresponded with us about "CJ," his resident feline:

The laws of evolution to the contrary notwithstanding, CJ has shown a distinct preference for low-protein foods such as potatoes over the soy he needs, whether as ground beans or as tofu. We seem finally to have had success with the *TVP* that is foisted off on humans in "vegetarian chili," etc. Perhaps he likes the (pardon the expression) "meaty" texture. Anyway, the Potato-Soy is now his favorite. Good thing, too, as he doesn't care much for lentils or any other kinds of beans, either. ... I refer to his wet food as "10 Lives" — nine for the cat and one for the cow whose life was spared.

Baby food

Many people tell about the convenience of baby food. Just add *Vegecat*, oil and yeast for a nutritious food. Traveling is easy

since baby foods don't require refrigeration and their small
portions make leftovers easier to store.

Some use them as a special treat, as Nancy Robinson related
from Maryland:

They love baby food (the good kind at 86¢ per jar!), especially sweet potatoes on top of the recipes. I use fresh veggies
most of the time, but use baby food for a treat. They also love
black eyed peas and margarine spread on veggies.

Seaweed

Since our supplements already contain seaweed, we were surprised when people added *more* to enhance palatability. It seems
cats are choosy when it comes to varieties of seaweed, and there's
room for experimentation. Canadian Pat Jones wrote:

Just wanted to drop a line in thanks for your help in con-
verting our cat to a totally vegetarian diet. It was certainly
above and beyond the call of duty to [come up with] all of
those recipes.

We have had success with a recipe involving mostly garbanzos, but the secret ingredient was seaweed, purchased in
an Oriental store and called nori. As I had been trying to convert her for almost a year, I was very relieved to find something that finally worked. As I'm sure you know, a battle of
wills with a cat can be a grueling experience.

As one of your common ordinary maudlin cat owners, I
would enclose a photo of mine, except I'm sure you have a
wall covered with them. Suffice it to say she is dear to me,
even more so as a vegetarian.

Veggie burger

Vegetarian burger preparations abound. Besides regional formulations, national companies jumping on this fast-moving
bandwagon make obtaining this popular food easier than ever.
The best veggie burgers for cats are based on wheat gluten, but
soy based preparations are also good — just higher in magnesium.

Depending upon how much oil the burger contains, it may be necessary to add more. For those containing safflower oil, add olive or another recommended oil, as well as nutritional yeast and supplement. Marsha Torr from Alabama wrote of her success:

We have been adopted by several stray cats, and as we are strict vegetarians, were delighted to discover your products two years ago. Our cats live on the mixture described [below], and are very healthy. The recipe is one that we evolved to as a variation of yours. They like it very much.

> 20 oz can of Worthington's *Vegeburger*
> One-half 20-ounce can garbanzos (blended)
> 8 heaped teaspoons quick oatmeal
> 10 teaspoons nutritional yeast
> 3½ teaspoons *Vegecat*
> 12 teaspoons peanut oil

Blend the garbanzos with a blender to a smooth paste (I include the liquids). Add the oatmeal and stir. Add the rest of the ingredients and mix thoroughly. Store in a sealed container in the refrigerator.

This makes enough for two medium cats for about two and one-half days. Serve with a little torn up seaweed on top.

Dry food

Cats raised on kibble may find home cooked recipes unfamiliar only because of the new texture and refuse to eat. Useful in that case are hard crackers commonly imported from Europe. Crumbled into the new food just prior to serving, they may make the transition easier, as well as helping teeth stay clean.

Jennifer Friedman writes of her experience:

I've discovered two tricks that might be useful for others. One is to add a few corn chips, broken up, to the food. The other is to cook much of the water out of the food (lentils and oats, for example). Add the tamari [soy sauce], oil, nutritional yeast, supplement, and veggies. Spread thinly on a cookie sheet. Bake on a low temperature until crisp. Then break into pieces. I usually serve this with a "side salad" of their favorite vegetables since it is cooked.

Temperature

Many experts state that food served at room temperature is more palatable than cold. This is because low temperatures lock in flavors. Heating makes volatile substances more aromatic.

Our cats are used to food served directly from the refrigerator with a fresh sprinkling of yeast flakes. Finicky Veggie seems to prefer his food cold, since that's the way he judges freshness. Food left over after a meal and not refrigerated, not only becomes drier but warmer as well. However, in the beginning, start with food that isn't too cold.

Creative challenge

Sometimes a little kitchen magic is what it takes. David Taylor talks about changing diets of stubborn animals:

If you inherit an old animal that is set in its ways, a little culinary effort may wrinkle it out of its determination to fast to death unless given a monotonous diet of crayfish or caviar.

Your cat will most likely learn to love simple food you prepare, but at first you may need enticements such as imitation bacon bits, "meat-flavored" broths and substitutes.

Spirulina

One of our cats thought spirulina (blue-green micro algae) was *ambrosia*. She taught me how much she loved it when I manufactured spirulina energy bars for another company. Batches were mixed in a 32-gallon container, and cleaning up involved taking the barrel outside on the lawn and hosing it down with water. Green spirulina froth ended up on the lawn. Priya (our calico) spent the next hour licking the lawn, obviously enjoying her spirulina feast. Since she loved it so much, I added it to her regular food, perking it up as well as adding valuable additional vitamins and minerals.

You may be surprised to find what your cat likes — perhaps pasta sauce or various cereals. A treat in summertime (and best served alone) is cantaloupe. Husk a freshly picked raw ear of corn, place it on your lawn and watch your cat go for it.

Frequency of feeding

Carnivores in nature have little control over timing and size of meals because their prey has to be located, stalked, hunted, and may not be easily captured. Considerable effort may be expended. Predacious creatures take infrequent large meals whenever opportunity arises. Like most carnivores, cats are opportunistic feeders. However, the advent of dry rations and never empty food bowls changed all that.

Given a free-feeding regime, cats adopt a nibbling food intake strategy with several small meals taken at random throughout day and night. One 1975 study found cats fed on this basis took 8-12 meals per day, predominantly at night. Another study, in 1982, found cats consuming between 7-16 meals per day. The size and timing of cats' meals were random.

The relationship between availability of food and the energy expended in obtaining that food affects feeding patterns. As the energy cost of obtaining a meal goes up, cats take fewer, larger, and slower meals per day (relative to free-feeding). This means that if your cat gets fed every time he or she walks into the kitchen, more and smaller meals result. If this isn't convenient for your schedule, then by all means reduce meals to as little as twice a day. Frequency and size of meals within these constraints have little bearing on health. Cats adapt to either way.

Kittens & queens need more...

Kittens (up to about 12 months) and queens have requirements different from adults. *Vegekit,* formulated especially for them, contains additional vitamin A, taurine, and arachidonic acid. If temporarily unable to obtain *Vegekit,* add an egg every other day to *Vegecat* recipes to come closer to growth requirements. Eggs are unnecessary with *Vegekit.*

Elderly Cats

Older cats require fewer calories, as well as less protein. See the section on elderly dogs in the next chapter.

FOR CONVENIENCE

It need not take more than ten to 15 minutes once a week for food preparation. Here's how to make a week's worth of the following recipe (Gentle Garbanzo):

⅝ cup (110g) cooked garbanzo beans (chick peas)
1.8 tbsp (24g) oil
1.8 tbsp (20g) yeast powder
1¹⁄₁₆ tsp (3.7g) *Vegecat*

Kitchen math

Multiply all measurements by seven (or 14 for two cats, etc.). In this case, choosing one week for one cat, we get seven times ⅝ which is ³⅝. Divide the 35 by eight to get four, leaving three. Therefore we need 4⅜ cups of cooked garbanzos.

$$7 \times \frac{5}{8} \text{ equals } \frac{35}{8} \text{ equals } 8\overline{)35} \begin{array}{r} 4 \\ \hline 35 \\ \underline{32} \\ 3 \end{array}$$

Next we need 7 times 1.8 tablespoons of oil:

$$7 \times 1.8 \text{ equals } \begin{array}{r} 1.8 \\ \underline{\times 7} \\ 12.6 \end{array}$$

Tablespoon/Cup Conversion

Tablespoons	Cup	Tablespoons	Cup
2	⅛	10	⅝
4	¼	12	¾
6	⅜	14	⅞
8	⅛	16	1
3 teaspoons is equal to 1 tablespoon			

From the chart above, 12.6 tablespoons is almost 13, between 12 and 14, or between the ¾ and ⅞ marks on a measuring cup. Rounding off to either mark is fine.

Go through the same process for yeast powder. If you have yeast flakes double the volume (not weight) measurement.

Next comes *Vegecat.* Using the same procedure as before, multiply seven times 11/16 teaspoon. This equals 77 sixteenths. Divide 77 by 16 to get four with 13 left over. That equals 4 13/16 teaspoons of *Vegecat.*

Converting Sixteenths

Sixteenths	Equals	Sixteenths	Equals
2	⅛	10	⅝
4	¼	12	¾
6	⅜	14	⅞
8	½	16	1

Thirteen-sixteeths of a teaspoons is almost ⅞ of a teaspoon, making it about 4⅞ teaspoons of *Vegecat.* Round it off to five level teaspoons — that's close enough.

The expanded recipe for one week looks like this:

    4⅜ cup (770g) cooked garbanzo beans (chick peas)

    ⅞ cup (168g) oil

    ⅞ cup (140g) yeast powder

    5 tsp (26g) *Vegecat*

Take the time to figure this out once, write down the measurements, and you'll not have to do it again.

Use the chart, "Preparing Grains & Legumes," in Chapter 7 for guidance in cooking beans. Since garbanzos double in volume when cooked, start with a little less than two and one-half cups of uncooked beans. Soak them for four hours (if longer they may ferment) and discard soak water. Add fresh water, covering beans one inch over the top and cook until soft in a partially covered pot. Stir occasionally for even cooking. Easier yet, use an electric crock pot, cooking beans at high temperature for at least part of the time. Beans are done when they mash easily.

Drain the water. Slightly crush the still warm beans with a potato masher. The hotter the beans the easier they are to crush. Cats like a little texture, so don't crush so thoroughly that they become paste. Add the other ingredients (nutritional yeast, oil, and *Vegecat)* as well as flavorings such as crushed peas and imitation bacon bits.

Store the food in small, convenient covered containers in the refrigerator. Serve small chunks in a clean bowl, coated with a sprinkling of nutritional yeast. Put leftover food back into the containers, maintaining freshness. If reserving food, "freshen" it up. Always have fresh, clean water available.

Feeding kittens and adults together

For cats under 12 months of age, use *Vegekit* and the recipes found later in this chapter, "Feeding Kittens." Sometimes it is impossible to separate cats at feeding time. In that case, feeding both of them with *Vegekit* recipes does no harm. However, to avoid over supplementation, we suggest limiting to one year the period *Vegekit* is fed adult cats.

How Much to Feed

Each recipe makes one day's food for a 10-pound (4.5kg) cat. Cats may eat more or less and still be normal. See the "Energy Requirements" chart in Chapter 6.

For lacto-ovo vegetarians, some recipes contain dairy products or eggs. Cats do just fine without those ingredients.

Precise measurements given in the recipes make for greater accuracy when multiplying portions for larger batches. At first, follow the recipes closely, learning proportions.

Don't add *Vegepet* supplements to nutritionally complete commercial pet foods as that would upset their nutrient balances.

Analyses are by dry weight basis. For a more comprehensive analysis see Appendix 2.

CAT RECIPES

1. GENTLE GARBANZO

⅝ cup (110g) cooked garbanzo beans (chick peas)
1.8 tbsp (24g) oil
1.8 tbsp (20g) yeast powder
1¹⁄₁₆ tsp (3.7g) *Vegecat*
Protein 20.5%, Fat 31.5%, Ash 3.4%, Mg .11%

2. COTTAGE GARBANZO

½ cup (110g) cooked garbanzo beans (chick peas)

½ cup (105g) cottage cheese

1.2 tbsp (16g) oil

1.4 tbsp (16g) yeast powder

1¹⁄₁₆ tsp (3.7g) *Vegecat*

Protein 29.8%, Fat 24.6%, Ash 4.2%, Mg .09%

3. EGGO-GARBANZO

⁷⁄₁₆ cup (85g) cooked garbanzo beans (chick peas)

1 large (50g) egg

1.5 tbsp (20g) oil

1.1 tbsp (12g) yeast powder

1¹⁄₁₆ tsp (3.7g) *Vegecat*

Protein 25.2%, Fat 33.0%, Ash 3.6%, Mg .10%

4. GLORIOUS GLUTEN

⁹⁄₁₆ cup (120g) wheat gluten

1.6 tbsp (22g) oil (less if gluten contains oil)

2.2 tbsp (24g) yeast powder

1¹⁄₁₆ tsp (3.7g) *Vegecat*

Protein 35.6%, Fat 30.2%, Ash 4.4%, Mg .07%

5. GENTLE LENTIL

¾ cup (115g) cooked lentils

1.6 tbsp (22g) oil

2.1 tbsp (24g) yeast powder

1¹⁄₁₆ tsp (3.7g) *Vegecat*

Protein 23.5%, Fat 27.8%, Ash 3.4%, Mg .10%

6. SOY OAT DELIGHT

⅜ cup (85g) cooked oats

1/8 cup (20g) textured vegetable protein

1.8 tbsp (16g) oil

1.8 tbsp (20g) yeast powder

11⁄16 tsp (3.7g) *Vegecat*

Protein 25.6%, Fat 32.8%, Ash 3.9%, Mg .14%

FEEDING KITTENS

Read the preceding sections since much of the information also applies to *Vegekit*. Switch to *Vegecat* supplement when your cat is about 12 months of age.

At a good age to carefully introduce new foods into their diet, just weaned kittens adjust to the vegetarian diet quite readily. David Taylor advises:

> Variety is the key principle to observe when feeding a cat. You should accustom a kitten to a wide variety of food from the day that it is weaned.

How Much to Feed

Each recipe makes one day's food for a 20-week-old, five-pound (2.2kg) kitten. To find out approximately how much to feed each day for various stages in your cat's growth, use the following table. Multiply portions in the recipes by the Factor indicated.

Adjust proportions for your cat. Cats may eat more or less than these portions and still be normal. Inactive cats eat considerably less and those exposed to cold weather eat more (see the "Energy Requirements" chart in Chapter 6).

Feline Growth

Age	Weight	Factor
10 weeks	2.2 lbs. (1kg)	0.9
20 weeks	4.9 lbs (2.2kg)	1.0
30 weeks	6.8 lbs. (3.1kg)	1.1
40 weeks	7.7 lbs. (3.5kg)	1.0
52 weeks	Switch to *Vegecat* QUEENS	
Gestation	10 lbs. (4.5kg)	1.6
Lactation	Feed as required	

⮂ KITTEN RECIPES ⮃

1. GENTLE GARBANZO

⅞ cup (150g) cooked garbanzo beans (chick peas)

2 tbsp (27g) oil

2¾ tbsp (29g) yeast powder

⅞ tsp (4g) *Vegekit*

Protein 21.7%, Fat 27.2%, Ash 3.9%, Mg .13%

2. COTTAGE GARBANZO

7/16 cup (80g) cooked garbanzo beans (chick peas)

7/16 cup (85g) cottage cheese

.8 tbsp (12g) oil

1¼ tbsp (14g) yeast powder

⅞ tsp (4g) *Vegekit*

Protein 30.1%, Fat 23.1%, Ash 4.7%, Mg .11%

3. EGGO-GARBANZO

⅜ cup (75g) cooked garbanzo beans (chick peas)

1 large egg (50g) cooked or raw

1 tbsp (14g) oil

1.1 tbsp (12g) yeast powder

⅞ tsp (4g) *Vegekit*

Protein 24.9%, Fat 30.9%, Ash 3.9%, Mg .11%

4. GLORIOUS GLUTEN

⁷⁄₁₆ cup (100g) wheat gluten

½ tbsp (16g) oil

1¾ tbsp (20g) yeast powder

⅞ tsp (4g) *Vegekit*

Protein 36.4%, Fat 27.6%, Ash 4.9%, Mg .08%

5. GENTLE LENTIL

½ cup (80g) cooked lentils

4 tsp (18g) oil

1¾ tbsp (20g) yeast powder

⅞ tsp (4g) *Vegekit*

Protein 23.4%, Fat 29.1%, Ash 3.9%, Mg .11%

6. SOY OAT DELIGHT

¼ cup (70g) cooked oats

⅛ cup (20g) textured vegetable protein

1¼ tbsp (16g) oil

1¾ tbsp (20g) yeast powder

⅞ tsp (4g) *Vegekit*

Protein 28.3%, Fat 26.7%, Ash 4.6%, Mg .16%

Kittens go vegetarian

Lil Frank wrote us from Minnesota:

PUMPKIN & WYLIE

They are both ten months old, very healthy, and have been vegetarians ever since I got them at ten weeks from the local animal shelter.

They really enjoy their food, their favorites being garbanzos, and rice and soy to which we add celery, green pepper, and kohlrabi (all steamed). I do sometimes add raw vegetables to their food, but not often enough unfortunately.

Tastier than commercial

Cecelia Schmieder, writing from Massachusetts related:

Our kitten, Griswel, enjoys her *Vegekit* meals much more than she ever did her dry commercial food, and who wouldn't prefer a diet of chickpeas and nutritional yeast, delicately seasoned with the finest olive oil, shoyu, etc., to a disgusting unidentifiable mixture of diseased chicken parts, moldy grains, propyl gallate, and so forth?

We find that she's more adventurous in food matters since switching over to a vegetarian diet. She used to only like sunflower seeds, raisins, and mushrooms. Now, she'll at least try anything that's not acidic or sour. She's been vegetarian now for about eight months, maybe nine, and is sleeker and healthier than ever.

Chapter 9

CANINE CHOW

D̂ogs along with wolves, jackals, and foxes are members of Canida, one of 10 families making up the order Carnivora (meaning flesh eaters). However some Carnivora (bears, raccoons, and the lesser panda found in the Himalayas) feed extensively on vegetable material.

Other members of Carnivora feed *exclusively* on fruit, such as the tree-dwelling kinkajou of tropical America. The catlike binturong of the civet family eats *mainly* fruit. Found in dense forests of southern Asia, Indonesia, and Malaysia, it weighs from 20 to 30 pounds, has long shaggy hair, tufted ears, a long bushy tail and *reportedly* makes an affectionate pet. Before any of you write HOANA and ask about binturongs, we haven't seen these animals in person, and have no idea about how or if it is even possible to obtain them in the United States.

Nutritionally omnivorous

Canine nutritional needs *can* be supplied by plants, but authorities advise at least some flesh. David Alderton studied veterinary medicine at Magdalene College, Cambridge, UK. As a consultant for the Pet Industry Joint Advisory Council he is a frequent contributor to periodicals. Asked whether dogs should be fed only on meat he answered in (1986) *The Dog Care Manual:*

No. In fact, dogs are less dependent on meat as the basis of their diet than cats are. A wide range of foods will keep your dog in good health; the main ingredients are the same as those which should be present in a human diet. Protein, comprised of various individual amino acids can be derived from either plant or animal sources.

Contradicting himself in the next sentence of the same paragraph, Alderton repeats the myth that dogs need animal protein:

The protein of plants lacks certain so-called essential amino acids, which should be present in the diet if a deficiency is not to occur.

Laboratories routinely maintain healthy dogs on purified diets containing *no* animal derived amino acids. *The Merck Veterinary Manual* states:

...Though classified as a carnivore, the dog utilizes a wide variety of foodstuffs efficiently. This ability enables the dog to meet his nutritional requirements from a remarkable diversity of diets. ...Some vegetable proteins are ... satisfactory sources of amino acids for dogs.

Small Animal Clinical Nutrition, a primary source book for many pet food manufacturers, states that, "Dogs are naturally omnivorous." To emphasize their point they compare Wyoming coyotes to their southern California counterparts. Whereas the first preys upon sheep, the latter plunders melons, peaches, apricots, grapes, plums, and cherries.

52 nutrients per ingredient

Formulating a vegetarian diet for a dog (or cat) consists of finding what is necessary for size, age and status (such as growth or pregnancy), and matching those specifics up with non-animal ingredients. HOANA combined natural ingredients, analyzed for 52 nutrients, into palatable recipes. What was missing, as far as meeting requirements, went into the supplements.

Getting started

By starting out with a relatively young dog, you'll probably have an easy time introducing the new food. For canines attached to one kind of food you may meet resistance just as with some cats (read Chapter 8).

This isn't because the food is vegetarian. Switching dogs to a homemade flesh-based diet, or simply a different brand of commercial food, often raises resistance. Dogs adept at using psychology to get their way have well trained masters. Sometimes dogs have to be really hungry to change their diet.

It is important that your dog eat enough of the food for good health. Don't let the dietary transition become a drawn out "battle of wills" with the dog starving because of your insistence.

Fixed food preference

Vets call attachment to a particular food a "fixed food preference." They recommend mixing in a small amount of the new food with the old food and adjusting the proportion over a period of days or weeks. See the preceding chapter for details.

Some dogs gobble their new food right from the start. Laura Moore wrote from Nevada:

Words cannot express my thankfulness and relief in finding your products! Feeding my cat and dog meat for the past year has been traumatic for me — and they (especially my dog) didn't seem to be enjoying it either. Every feeding time was filled with dread.

I tried lots of brand name combinations and my dog (15 pounds) steadily refused to get excited about any of it (except when she was raiding the cat bowl!).

Your product is a god-send! She (the dog) immediately became interested in her food as never before and even began asking for seconds! The tom-cat didn't miss a beat... It's thrilling. As a devout vegetarian, I can now feel satisfied at being a conscious pet owner.

More hints

Since dogs love meat flavor, use something like a vegetarian ham soup base as a substitute for salt called for in the recipes. Commercial companies add meat flavors, cheese flavors, smokes, mint, bacon, onion and garlic flavors. Health food stores have similar products for vegetarians. One readily available flavoring is imitation bacon bits.

Commercial dog food often contains digest (see Appendix 1). Dogs go crazy for it and there's no exact vegetarian equivalent. But try to find foods of vegetarian origin that your dogs really like. It may take some detective work. Leanda Barr, living in Pennsylvania discovered an algae right on her own land:

They [our dogs] love bananas, watermelon, grapes, cantaloupe, blueberries and peaches. I mash or puree the fruit so they get all the nutrients out of them. My *Cuisinart* is getting used for them more than for me.

We live on 10 acres so there is plenty of grass for them to graze on. They especially like what grows around the pond. My husband scooped the algae out of the pond one evening. They went crazy over it. I let them eat it because I felt it was right.

Does your dog like pasta sauce, or cereals? Try putting a fresh, raw ear of corn on your lawn and see if your dog relishes it.

The "Crackers" recipe is nutritionally complete, good for leaving out for extended periods, convenient for feeding by others, and handy for traveling.

Obesity

Obesity is the most common nutritional disease occurring in the dog, affecting 25-40 percent of all dogs in the United States. Aged dogs and spayed females are especially prone to this problem. Health problems related to obesity include impaired cardiac function, respiratory disorders, heat stress, and skin problems. Veterinarian Gregory MacEwen states, "Obesity can be one of the major conditions which can adversely affect the longevity of a pet."

People just starting their animals on this diet will be relieved to find that obesity is usually not a problem. Without tantalizing commercial concoctions such as "digest" (see Appendix 1) dogs eat for bodily needs instead of titillating their palate.

Reasons for overeating (the most common cause for obesity) include boredom, idleness, nervousness, and conditioning. For a few, there may be physiological problems such as hormonal imbalances and if suspected, go to a veterinarian for diagnosis.

Caloric restrictions along with more exercise are the most effective ways to manage obesity. Avoiding treats, decreasing oil in recipes, and smaller meals fed more often are effective tools for weight reduction. If possible, keep your canine companion out of the kitchen during food preparation, minimizing anxiety.

Older Dogs

For nutritional purposes most dogs should be considered aged at seven years and giant breeds, aged at five years. Reduce the protein and sodium (salt) intake due to renal and cardiovascular changes. Protein intake can be lowered by cutting back on legumes, or using lentils instead of garbanzos. Small, frequent meals may also be necessary.

Administer a low potency adult multivitamin pill daily. Probably the vitamins C and E will still be inadequate. For Vitamin C recommendations see Chapter 6. Wendell Belfield recommends 100-200 IU vitamin E for each 22 pounds of your dog's weight to a maximum of 800 IU.

Amount to Feed Dogs

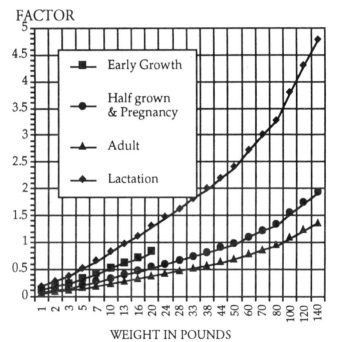

WEIGHT IN POUNDS

For convenience, make a large quantity of food at a time. See Chapter 8 for detailed instructions.

Each recipe makes one day's food for an adult 88-pound (40kg) dog. Use the above chart for modifying recipe measurements (except for *Vegedog*) for your dog's weight and stage in life.

Compute Vegedog amount separately

Compute the daily requirement for *Vegedog* by taking a recipe's measurement and multiplying by factor indicated in the following table. For example, a 45-pound dog gets .5 times one tablespoon *Vegedog*, or ½ tablespoon per day. A 90-pound dog gets 1.2 times a tablespoon of *Vegedog,* which is about one and one-fourth tablespoon. Do this math once and write it down for future reference. At first, follow the recipes closely to learn proportions. Making the recipes will become second nature with time.

Amount of *Vegedog*

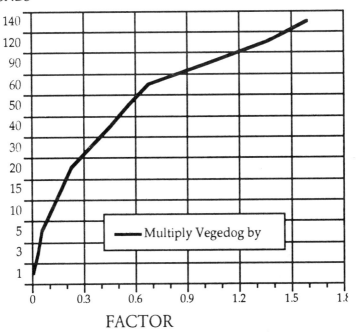

POUNDS

FACTOR

Just like people, dogs enjoy fresh food and it's better for them. Refrigerate leftover food in covered containers. Freshen up leftovers by stirring or adding sprouts, shredded carrots, or other vegetables. Fresh water must always be available.

Analyses are by dry weight basis. See Appendix 2 for details.

DOG RECIPES

1. GENTLE GARBANZO

8 cups (1600g) cooked garbanzo beans (chick peas)

5 tbsp (64g) oil

2¼ tbsp (24g) yeast powder

1 tbsp (17g) *Vegedog*

¼ tsp (1g) salt

Protein 19.4%, Fat 12.2%, Fiber 5.2%

2. COTTAGE GARBANZO

7½ cups (1360g) cooked garbanzo beans (chick peas)

¾ cup (185g) cottage cheese

5 tbsp (64g) oil

2½ tbsp (29g) yeast powder

1 tbsp (17g) *Vegedog*

Protein 21.9%, Fat 14.1%, Fiber 4.7%

3. SOY OAT DELIGHT

6 ¼ cups (1840g) cooked oats

1 cup (136g) textured vegetable protein

6 tbsp (80g) oil

3¼ tbsp (35g) yeast powder

1 tbsp (17g) *Vegedog*

¼ tsp (1g) salt

Protein 21.4%, Fat 19.0%, Fiber 3.3%

4. EGGO SOY

3¾ cup (500g) textured vegetable protein

4 tbsp (55g) oil

2 large eggs (100g)

1½ tbsp (16g) yeast powder

1 tbsp (17g) *Vegedog*

¼ tsp (1g) salt

Protein 20.3%, Fat 12.5%, Fiber 5.1%

5. COTTAGE SOY

3¾ cup (500g) textured vegetable protein

3¾ tbsp (50g) oil

1½ cup (185g) cottage cheese

1½ tbsp (16g) yeast powder

1 tbsp (17g) *Vegedog*

Protein 21.8%, Fat 11.0%, Fiber 5.0%

6. CRUNCHY CRACKERS

1⅓ cup (250g) whole wheat flour

½ cup (67g) textured vegetable protein

1½ tbsp (19g) oil

1¾ tbsp (20g) yeast powder

1 tbsp (17g) *Vegedog*, ¼ tsp (1g) salt

Protein 21.2%, Fat 7.8%, Fiber 2.0%

Gradually add water to above ingredients (and favorite seasonings) to make a stiff dough. Knead until dough is smooth and pliable. Roll on floured surface to one-fourth to one-half inch thickness. Cut out like cookies, place on oiled baking sheet. Bake at 325° for 30 minutes (or until lightly browned). Leave in warm oven (with door slightly open) overnight to become hard.

Chapter 10

HUNTING

Love to eat them mousies,
mousies what I love to eat.
Bite they little heads off...
nibble on they tiny feet.

Kliban: *Momcat*

Karen Talberth, in Oregon, wrote:

As a vegetarian owner of two cats, I always feel sad at best, hypocritical at worst, when I feed them meat. I have always thought that it was necessary; I read once that if you withdraw meat from their diet, they will just go hunting to make up for it. Since they already hunt, I wouldn't want to increase their activity.

There is no relationship between the need to kill and the need to eat. Experiments comparing kittens whose sole solid food consisted of prey animals to those who had never tasted raw meat showed that although both groups hunted equally, the latter group, even when hungry, didn't make the connection between killing and eating. Other research demonstrated no difference in killing between hungry cats and those just fed.

Killer cats

Designed as an efficient killing machine, cats *are* carnivorous in their natural feeding behavior. Their play revolves around crouching, springing, and catching anything that moves. The poem at the beginning of this chapter accurately describes cat nature. Feral cats eating only mice consume 12 per day, often starting with the head!

Wildlife lovers shudder at the loss of wildlife from killer cats. Cats kill, according to a University of Wisconsin study, an estimated one million songbirds each year in the United States. Estimates of rabbits killed each year run as high as 47 million. Severe predation on mice and voles may also affect the survival of birds of prey, such as owls and hawks.

Hunting is learned

How a cat starts life has a lot to do with his behavior later on. If you have a choice, find kittens exposed from birth to people and hands, and preferably not exposed to hunting. It stands to reason that a strictly indoor queen will not be so keen on teaching its babies to hunt. David Taylor reports:

Feline hunting actions aren't instinctive; they are learned from other cats. So kittens that are born to non-hunting mothers, or lack litter-mates, don't learn to hunt.

If the mother cat is going to teach her kittens to hunt, it's during the sixth to 20th weeks of their life. If untaught after this point, kittens may learn to kill later, but only with much greater difficulty. The sight of live prey is not thought to be enough to incite untaught kittens to kill. Kittens initially may be frightened by prey animals and their attempts to escape, since the connection between "food" and a live animal is not readily apparent. Mother cats bring injured prey to her kitten, not as toys, but to teach this connection.

Pecking order

Position in litter may have some bearing on the ease with which a kitten learns to kill. Higher ranking kittens learn faster. In play, the nape bite is too dangerous a tool to be used except in earnest. Some kittens do it correctly from the start. Subordinate kittens in a litter may not have enough strength to bite into a mouse's neck with enough force to kill it. Afterwards, they may never work up enough courage to be an efficient killer, preferring wads of paper over prey.

Individual cats, for whatever reason, sometimes have no urge to chase and kill its normal prey. Aside from that, females are *the* hunters in the cat family, and they prefer hunting at night. Male lions sometime help, but only to frighten prey into an ambush by females. The burden of killing falls to the lioness, not to His Majesty. If you have a choice between a male or a female cat, that may be something to consider.

No meat Veggie

Veggie has been vegetarian ever since Kumari brought her friend home in January 1986 to share her vegan dog food (the first stray we'd seen in six years). He was about five or six months old, and immediately ate vegan food, preferring us instead of the neighbor, who supplied kibble for neighborhood strays.

We keep our cats indoors at night. It works two ways. Not only does it cut down on hunting, but it prevents our cats from being prey to Dangerous Creatures (such as coyotes we hear occasionally in the early morning hours, sometimes *very* close).

The other night my wife let Veggie out later than usual, thinking he would come right back in as he always does. Ebony stayed inside, not given the chance to go out so late. This time, however, Veggie didn't come back when she called his name.

At four-thirty the next morning a very concerned Kathi opened the door and there was Veggie, coming in after stepping over a mouse he'd killed (not eaten). Veggie's the pacifist among the pawed ones. As far as we knew, this was the first time in over a year that he had actually killed a mouse.

Later, Kathi let both cats out into the fresh morning. Ebony likes to move fast, and as first lady, led the way — speeding through the door but she *screeched* to a halt when she spied the mouse on the doormat. Bouncing back, she grabbed the dead mouse and hissed her warning to Veggie, "Stay away!" He totally ignored her, as he is wont to do when she gets too feisty, and nonchalantly walked past her into the yard.

This seems to support a note in *Cat Catalog* that, "Cats raised on a vegetarian diet will still hunt and kill prey if they get the chance, although they are less likely to eat what they catch."

Ebony is a fair weather cat who stays in when it snows or rains. She doesn't like to walk in the white stuff. She *does* hunt during the warm months. We know, since her favorite place to eat prey is on the front doormat after which she wants to come in, scratching at the door until we open it. Then she makes a bee-line for her food bowl. Dutifully we take out garbanzo food. Maybe it gets rid of mouse breath.

Veggie doesn't disappear from sight when he's outside. Usually he stays in plain view, browsing on grass, doing his toilet, sun bathing, and generally being lazy. As a vegetarian for more than six years, he prefers garbanzo beans to fresh mouse.

Inside cats

Some, when given the choice, prefer keeping their cats inside. This isn't unreasonable, as Cecelia Schmieder recounted:

Griswel was raised an indoor cat. Contrary to what many people say about indoor cats, she is not bored or destructive or

overweight. In fact, when we try to take her for walks outdoors, she is bored, and uncomfortable. An open window is as
close to nature as she feels need to be. I don't think this is
perverse or unnatural or anything, and it saves her from getting run over by cars or killing and eating other animals, who
might also have poison in their systems. I thought I'd let you
know as one more small piece of evidence that cats don't have
to be "completely free and wild" to be happy.

Friendly enemies

Predator and prey friendships occasionally occur, sharing the
same food dish, etc. These alliances between natural enemies are
tricky to establish and may be dangerous, although sometimes
they are maintained successfully as with Socks and Mr. Bunny in
Chapter 4.

German researcher Paul Leyhausen reported that his cat Tilly,
whose diet included live rats, made friends with one of them. One
rat managed to escape being a meal by hiding under Tilly's
sleeping box, making forays into her cage and even nipping at
Tilly's heels until she gave it the run of the cage. She went about
killing other rats, but never made the mistake identifying her
"pet" rat for one of them. She even shared her fresh-killed rats
with her now cannibalistic friend.

The two slept together, with Tilly holding the rat to her
breast with her paws. They were inseparable for four months, after which Leyhausen took the rat away. Three months later he returned it to her cage. Tilly showed no signs of recognition and
started after it. The rat jumped into Tilly's sleeping box. But it
was of no use. Tilly leaped into the box and ate her former friend.

Chapter 11

OBJECTIONS

e received the following letter from J.W.:

A vegetarian diet for cats is sick! What does it prove? That humans have dominion over animals? Certainly no person with so much love for animals [that] they abhor their slaughter is trying to prove that. Vegetarians certainly have no right to invade that animal's privacy by forcing it to live on a diet that's clearly unnatural for the species. They will only develop eye problems, blindness, and most likely die from a vegetable diet (even with taurine added). Why make them miserable?

Dick Gregory, the timeless comedian turned pacifist, writes:

People are funny about their pets and their pets' diet. When you suggest to some folks that they ought to try putting their dogs and cats on a meatless diet, they will respond as though their little pets had never been domesticated! They will say, "Dogs and cats are supposed to eat meat. After all, they're descended from tigers and wolves!" Of course, if there was any real practicing line of descent, the chances are the pets would already have consumed their owners and their owners' kids!

Before we sold the *Sun Bar* business, our clientele consisted of
many vegetarians who shunned flesh for health reasons, rather
than concern for animals marching to the slaughterhouses. One
of the projects on the drawing board (which never got off the
ground) was a book promoting raw food. When we started re-
searching vegetarianism for cats, some of our customers felt we
had abandoned them. G.S. wrote :

> You go off on a tangent with cats when humans, especial-
> ly senior citizens, could be extending their life span with in-
> formation and encouragement about live foods. Fortunately, a
> book called *Raw Energy* from Australia is available. I would
> have been a regular customer of your *Sun Bars* ...if you had
> exhibited the same concern for humans as ugh! — cats!
>
> Now get angry with me for daring to tell you the truth
> [about] how your customers feel about your cat experiment.

We didn't get angry with G.S. As long time vegetarians we
were used to being at odds with those around us. We felt that our
original research would bring integrity and harmony into the lives
of the many ethical vegetarians with companion animals. By successfully shattering that last link to meat, we could do our bit at
closing slaughterhouses, with no possibility that animal companions in our care might be stranded for food.

Others have questioned us about "forcing" this dietary
change on carnivorous beings, going against their born nature.
Dick Gregory answers:

> ...Some pet owners, who would object to the killing of an-
> imals for the human diet, justify their purchasing meat from
> the butcher for their pets' consumption because the pets are
> natural carnivores. So they feed their pets beef, horse meat,
> pork, lamb, liver and all other forms of butcher shop raw
> meat. But that is not the *natural* raw meat diet of the carnivo-
> rous pet! To be consistent, such a pet owner would feed a dog
> raw rabbit, or chicken, or any of the small animals or birds
> the pet would naturally seize as prey.

Sometimes a pet owner will rationalize, "I tried giving my pet fruits and vegetables and more natural foods, but it preferred the canned pet food." It never seems to occur to the pet owner that the dog would prefer to relieve itself on the carpet, and would probably prefer *not* to roll over and play dead! Pet owners think nothing of housebreaking a dog, or training it to do tricks or to attack unwanted visitors; in short, to do things for the owner's benefit. But the same owner resists changing a pet's diet for the pet's benefit, and training the pet to eat it!

FROM EXPERTS

Lin, who you met in Chapter 6, wrote to *The Cat* magazine and asked for their opinion of the vegetarian diet she fed her cats. Mark Sunlin wrote back and Lin sent HOANA a copy of his reply. In turn we wrote to the editor, responding point by point:

Mr. Sunlin: Although the *Vegepet* company she now deals with claims to add a taurine supplement "from non-animal sources," *The Merck Index*, a 1700-page listing of chemicals, states that taurine is extracted commercially from ox bile.

HOANA: Mr. Sunlin uses very old reference materials. It is true that taurine formerly was first isolated from ox bile in 1827. In 1918, taurine came from the large muscle of abalone. Inorganic synthesis of taurine from 2-n bromoethanesulfonate dates back to 1930. Since 1947 the most economical method of obtaining taurine is synthesis by sodium sulfite sulfonation of ethylene chloride, followed by ammonolysis with anhydrous ammonia, or with aquas ammonia and ammonium carbonate. This method describes the process from which we obtain taurine. Cat food manufacturers use synthetic taurine in their products for economic reasons.

Mr. Sunlin: Even if it is obtainable from other sources *Vegepet* does not state at what levels it is added to their product, and this could be vital. For example, the heart-disease DCM associated with taurine deficiency was seen in cats consuming 25 to 50 mg of taurine per three and one-half ounce of dry food, while on a similar dry basis the whole-prey-mammal carcasses consumed by the ancestors of cats and dogs contained a massive 610mg, about 20 times the level associated with heart disease. Thus it is not enough that a product "contains taurine," it must contain high levels of taurine.

HOANA: Most commercial cat foods manufactured in the USA do not state what potency of taurine they contain. However, it is well known that they use the recommendations of the Committee on Animal Nutrition of the National Research Council. The majority of commercial cat foods are based primarily on plant sources with the addition of animal fat, animal by-products, and supplemented with vitamins, minerals and amino acids (including the sub-amino acid taurine). The *Vegecat* diet exceeds the minimum requirement for taurine, although it does not contain the levels recommended by Mr. Sunlin. No commercial foods do, unless they are 100% meat. Current labels on *Vegecat* clearly state the amount of taurine contained (487mg per ounce). There is absolutely no scientific evidence that cats require more than 800mg taurine per kg dry weight, the amount included in *Vegecat* diets.

Mr. Sunlin: Vegepet also makes rash claims about beneficial "enzymes" present in the raw eggs which it endorses, although enzymes, being proteins, are destroyed by digestive processes. While this means little in itself, it does cast suspicion on other claims made by the company.

HOANA: Mr. Sunlin misses the entire point of raw (enzyme rich) food, as well as being in error. Work at Northwestern University, published in the *Journal of Nutrition* by Ivy, Schmitt, and Beazell, showed that 51% of the malt amylase, an enzyme produced by germinating barley, passed into the intestine in active form, after it had digested starch in the stomach. Raw food supplies its own digestive enzymes. The raw egg alluded to contains the enzymes tributyrinase, lipase, phosphatase, peptidase, peroxidase, catalase, oxidase, and amylase. Consumers must supply missing enzymes for cooked food. Dogs and cats eating a natural raw food diet have no enzymes in their saliva. When fed cooked food, enzymes show up in the saliva within a week. These digestive enzymes use vital energy that would have been available for manufacturing hundreds of other enzymes necessary for life. Dr. Edward Howell, author of *Enzyme Nutrition* (700 pages long with 700 references to scientific literature), states that the length of life is inversely proportional to the rate of exhaustion of the enzyme potential of an organism.

Mr. Sunlin: Authorities generally recommend that feline diets contain less than .1% magnesium on a dry basis for all cats to prevent FUS....A whole-prey diet contains only .08% magnesium on a dry basis, while *Vegepet*'s recipes yield .15% magnesium on a moist basis, which is probably at least twice this high on a dry level. This is much too high, and is typical of vegetarian diets.

HOANA: Again Mr. Sunlin is in error, at least as to how much magnesium on a dry basis is contained in the *Vegecat* diet. Our literature clearly states that magnesium figures are on a dry basis (as they always have been). The recipes range from .07% to .14%. Previously they ranged from .07% to .19%, and we advised those who suspected that their cats were prone to FUS to choose lower magnesium recipes. Our experience with one cat experiencing FUS was total recovery within two weeks merely by switching from a .19% recipe to a .15% recipe (currently .11% due to a reformulation).

Mr. Sunlin: Cats also cannot utilize linoleic acid, the main component of most vegetable oils; more than useless, such unsaturated oils have been associated with cancer formation in humans and other mammals.

HOANA: Again Mr. Sunlin is in error, this time wildly so. For cats, linoleic acid (18:2n6), is an *essential* fatty acid. It has not been shown to cause cancer in dogs or cats at the levels found in our diets. One starts to wonder if Mr. Sunlin has done his research!

Mr. Sunlin: Many vegetarians or manufacturers of vegetarian petfoods maintain that dogs are omnivores, rather than carnivores, with the implication that they can easily switch to a vegetarian diet, and that cats can't be too far behind. ...It is

very probably that numerous dietary components not yet recognized as such exist in the cat's and dog's natural carnivorous
diet which are not present at sufficient levels, if at all, in non-
meat diets. The hope that one can recognize and replace these
is forlorn and unrealistic at best...

HOANA: Canis Familiaris (domestic dog), is considered nutritionally omnivorous because there has been no proof to the
contrary. Non-animal sources supply his every nutritional requirement, just as for humans. Considering the precarious
shape of our biosphere, it obviously behooves us to eat plant
rather than animal proteins that in their procurement
ultimately poison the earth. This is so well documented that
it belabors the point to dwell on it. The same applies for our
pets. If possible, we do well to convert from an omnivorous
diet to one based entirely on plants, with insufficient or
missing nutrients supplied from non-animal sources.

Mr. Sunlin's states that attempting to eliminate animal
products from pet food is "forlorn and unrealistic." He appears
to have no regard for the 2,200,000,000 pounds of cattle, sheep,
fish, and chickens packaged last year as "pet food" in this
country. Those billions of pounds put an incredible drain on
ecological resources, consuming billions more pounds of valuable grains and other foodstuffs. It seems worthwhile to find a
way of eliminating such a blight of suffering and destruction.

Aside from that, some dogs are allergic to beef. Also,
many older dogs suffer from seriously impaired kidney function and a large part of the problem is the prolonged overload
on kidneys handling wastes from meat.

Many veterinarians endorse supplemented, scientifically
formulated vegetarianism for pets as a healthy alternative to
the commercial pet foods which result in the spectrum of diseases seen every day in practice.

Mr. Sunlin needs to open his mind, weighing the advantages that accrue to a vegetarian diet, not only for people, but
also for pets. We challenge him to find one real fault to the
vegetarian diet for pets that we have so carefully researched
and presented, since 1986, to thousands of people the world

over. Our files bulge with letters attesting to the success of vegetarian diets over the alternative.

After responding to Mr. Sunlin's objections, and sending a copy of that response to Lin, she wrote again:

I ...was delighted when, last week, I received a copy of your letter to *The Cat*. I am writing in order to thank you for the time and trouble taken in responding to Mr. Sunlin's objections. I realize how precious your time is. As a lay person, I was completely baffled by science, when reading his paper, and found his response, at best, unhelpful. However, I was able to pick up on his apparent complete disregard for all those sentient creatures exploited, day in day out, worldwide, in order to satisfy the greed of the human animal and its pets! One of your paragraphs, in particular, crystallized my feelings and I thank you for putting it across so eloquently.

The two cats, with whom I share my life, continue to thrive on a *Vegecat* vegetarian diet: Tuppence, now 14 years old, and Kelly, almost eight. I'm now able to purchase *Vegecat* from the Vegan Society, here in the UK. Until recently I have had to make do with brewer's yeast as part of their diet, but have at last found a supplier of nutritional yeast flakes.

Thank you for caring.

Periodical pessimists

In 1986 HOANA phoned Dr. James Morris, telling him that we were developing a supplement for vegetarian cats. At that time he was encouraging and shared his views about what he thought was essential in the formulation. In particular, referring to taurine, he suggested a minimum of 800mg per kg diet, higher than the official NRC recommendation of 500mg per kg diet. Our first *Vegecat* formulation therefore contained 800mg per kg diet, and our customers avoided the 1987 cardiomyopathy panic associated with inadequate taurine levels.

Yet, in the *New York Times,* Morris goes on record against feline vegetarianism, ignoring our efforts (of which he was a part):

Q. *Could a healthy vegetarian diet be devised for cats?*

A. "Definitely not," said Prof. James Morris of the Department of Physiological Science at the School of Veterinary Medicine of the University of California at Davis.

After stating "definitely not," note how Morris hedges his bet:

A vegetable-based diet could be devised, he said, but only if some chemical reagents and animal fats were added to it. That is because cats cannot synthesize some of the essential fatty acids found in animal fat.

"For example, plants have virtually none of an amino acid called taurine," he said. "Taurine deficiency results in blindness and loss of hearing, dilated cardiomyopathy, grave retardation in kittens and the birth of kittens with developmental abnormalities."

Considering our prior conversations with Dr. Morris, it's difficult to understand his continued advice against vegetarianism. He (and others) seem duty bound to parrot the official line.

The President of the Massachusetts Society for the Prevention of Cruelty to Animals, Gus W. Thornton, DVM, answered the following question in *Animals:*

Q. Can cats be vegetarians? I am a vegetarian and want my cats to be too, but I also want them to be healthy. Is this possible? If so, what should I feed them?

A. Sometimes vegetarians want their pets to eat as they do. Meat-free prepared diets are commercially available or can be made at home. Examples of commercially available diets for dogs are Hills *Canine Prescription Diet k/d, dry u/d, dry d/d, and dry s/d.*

While it is difficult to develop a balanced vegetarian diet for dogs, it is impossible for cats to have a balanced diet that is free of all animal products (milk and eggs for example).

No wonder vegetarians give up on feeding cats a meatless diet! Experts, almost universally condemning vegetarianism for cats, state it so definitely that further inquiry is squashed.

Cats Magazine

The following editorial is from the April 1990 *CATS Magazine.*

VEGGIES NOT A STAPLE

We have received numerous letters from readers commenting that the humans in the household are vegetarians and inquiring whether or not that type of diet is feasible for the family cat.

Many vegetarians assume it is adequate, for if human life can be sustained and prosper without proteins derived from meat, why not cats?

The answer is no. Cats cannot be maintained, much less thrive on a protein deficient diet. Normally (unless under a special diet for medical reasons) a cat requires twice or three times as much protein as other species for the same level of growth and metabolism.

The type of protein required by the cat is equally as important as the amount, based on its amino acid composition. Two amino acids are essential to the cat. The cat cannot synthesize either one. They are taurine and arginine. The cat needs these continually because while most other species shut off the enzyme system that turns amino acids into energy, the cat does not. They consume part of their dietary protein for energy, rather than for tissue buildup. Thus the need for a high protein intake.

Another reason cats cannot join their human counterparts in a strictly vegetarian diet involves their need for vitamin A. Cats cannot convert beta-carotene into vitamin A. They do not have the enzyme system needed to utilize the vitamin A from plants. Cats also do not have the ability to take any source of vitamin A and convert it to their required preformed status.

In the wild, cats meet their vitamin A needs from eating other animals who have made their own vitamin A. For our domestic cats, their vitamin A needs are met with the liver in commercial cat foods.

While vegetarianism may become the choice for humans, it is absolutely unfeasible to include the cat in this dietary choice.

This editorial provoked a response from users of *Vegecat* in Holland, and the magazine printed Arlette's letter in the "Sound Off Cat Lovers" section of their August 1991 issue:

PRO VEGGIES

The April 1990 *CATS* editorial stated that it was not possible to have vegetarian cats. "Veggies Not A Staple," explained that cats need two amino acids, taurine and arginine, which they cannot synthesize, and vitamin A because they cannot convert beta-carotene into vitamin A.

Being a vegetarian who is against killing animals for any reason, I did not get any cats until I could find a way of raising them the vegetarian way while keeping them healthy.

Last summer in Hawaii, I contacted a vegetarian veterinarian, Ihor Basko, DVM. He recommended I read *Dogs & Cats Go Vegetarian* by Barbara Lynn Peden. In this book the author explains ...research into a vegetarian diet for cats and dogs. In fact, the entire research was based on finding a replacement for meat that would supply cats and dogs with taurine, arginine, vitamin A and the proper fats they need, without using any animal products.

I contacted the company that sells this supplement and ordered a supply.

My two kittens are eight months old now, have been vegans since birth, and are extremely healthy. They eat what I eat (beans, tofu, grains, vegetables, etc.), along with oil, brewer's yeast and the Harbinger's supplement that contains all they need plus many other vitamins. My cats are playful, full of energy, have beautiful fur and are the right weight. I am very happy that it is not necessary to take the life of a farm animal to sustain the life of my pets.

Arlette Liwer — Holland

Years ago experts told vegetarians that it was impossible to raise children on a vegetarian diet. That didn't work, so now experts stress the impossibility of vegetarian diets for cats.

The original *CATS Magazine* editorial gave as reasons for not feeding cats vegetarian:

1) Protein is quantitatively deficient

2) Two essential proteins for the cat (arginine and taurine) are unavailable from non-animal sources

3) Cats need non-vegetarian preformed vitamin A

In answer to the first objection, adequate protein is easily available in many vegetarian diets.

Objection two is only partially true. Arginine, while not an essential amino acid for humans, *is* for cats. However, arginine is *abundant* in plant proteins. Taurine *is* non-existent in foods of non-animal origin, but synthesized taurine is readily available.

Item three is true, but again, synthesized preformed vitamin A, either palmitate or acetate, is readily available.

Beyond natural

By observation and practical experience we've accumulated a large database of empirical evidence successfully supporting *supplemented* vegetarianism for cats. This confirmation becomes more indomitable with each year that passes.

In 1986, we visited with Richard Pitcairn, well known author and holistic veterinarian, and talked with him about the first edition of *Dogs & Cats Go Vegetarian*. He seemed helpful, pointing out possible improvements, and found no fault with our basic research. However, interviewed by Katherine Diehl in the September-October 1992 issue of *Body Mind & Spirit,* he "urges pet owners not to try 'imposing' an eggless, dairyless vegetarian diet on their dogs or cats. Nutrients animals need would be lacking."

Diehl goes on to say that holistic animal health consultants and vets "point out that any reliable taurine supplement comes from animals anyway." *What?* Pet food companies use the *same* synthetic taurine that we use, made from chemicals, not animals.

Diehl quotes Anitra Frazier, author of *The New Natural Cat:*

> If you're a vegetarian who can't handle feeding your cat meat, give the cat away. On a vegetarian diet, first they go blind, then they die.

Diehl continues in her article, "The Natural Animal," by relating Frazier's answer when asked about using supplements to replace meat in the diet. Frazier replied, "Say that I fell down and was kicking my arms and legs at the mere thought of it!"

That's probably a good place to leave both Pitcairn and Frazier. Some, in spite of irrefutable facts, refuse a higher path.

DIGEST VEGETABLES?

Dina Smithson wrote us from Louisiana:

> Q. Dear Harbingers: I read your book on vegetarian diets for dogs and cats. As vegan "parents" to seven dogs and one cat, my husband and I are very happy to provide our pets with healthy cruelty-free foods as recommended in your book.
>
> We are also teachers and public speakers, and we share vegan information with many people, some who are inspired to become vegetarians or vegans. Your book has provided even more information that we can now share! There is one question, however, which some people have asked us, and we do not yet have a clear answer for it. The question concerns the length of intestines of dogs and cats and their ability to assimilate vegetable matter in the most physiologically efficient way.
>
> For instance, one of the explanations that my husband and I give to people who do not understand why a vegetarian diet is healthier for humans than a meat diet, is that we as humans have long intestines. And like other animals with long

intestines, our bodies digest plant food most efficiently. Flesh has a tendency to putrefy in long intestines, ultimately contributing to the occurrence of many diseases, one of which is color cancer. Humans can survive eating a flesh-based diet, even though it is not the healthiest nor the most efficient diet for the human body.

So, the basic question that I am posing is about the converse of the above mentioned statements... what about cats and dogs with shorter intestines? Would not a primarily flesh-based diet with perhaps some herbs and vegetables be better for them since short intestines are designed for quick passage of digested material?

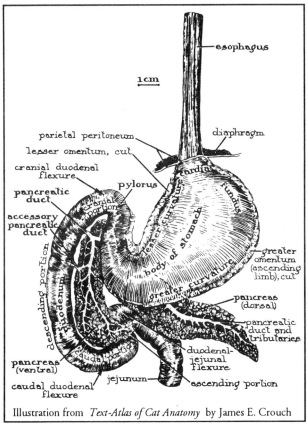

Illustration from *Text-Atlas of Cat Anatomy* by James E. Crouch

Dina stated, "Personally, we are convinced that a cruelty-free vegetable-based diet is not only healthier than the 'junk food' meat alternatives derived from factory farms, but it is better for our planet's spiritual growth and physical survival."

Carnivores have short intestines compared to other animals, but studies prove that cats (and dogs) readily digest cooked (or sprouted) non-animal foods. Studies in 1947 found that the apparent digestibility of proteins in an all vegetable diet containing white bread, corn, rice, potatoes, tomatoes, and applesauce was 80 percent. A 1980 study report apparent digestibility values of soybean meal, corn, rice and oats to be in the range of 77 to 88 percent, compared to the apparent digestibility values of 50 percent for meat and bone meal, 78 percent for beef, and 79 percent for liver. Commercial pet foods rely heavily upon plant sources.

PLANT ESTROGENS

At the 600-acre Wildlife Safari located at Winston, Oregon, I stood in awe a few feet away from a cheetah. Her luminous eyes stared into mine — predator and prey face to face. Even though protected by a secure barrier, this magnificent animal unnerved me enough that feelings of trepidation ruined the moment.

Racing towards extinction

A rate of acceleration comparable to that of a high-powered sports car (up to 60-70 mph), makes cheetahs the fastest animals in the world. Ten thousand years ago several cheetah species lived in North America, Europe, Asia and Africa. All became extinct except for today's cheetah, listed as endangered. It has disappeared from Asia, from India (last seen there in 1948), from Iran in the 1970s, and is nearly extinct in Africa. Population estimates vary between 5,000 and 25,000 worldwide.

Unusual among big cats, today's cheetahs are virtually geneti-
cally identical. This lack of genetic versatility is blamed for an epi-
demic of feline infectious peritonitis (FIP) that destroyed 17 cheetahs, half of those at the Wildlife Safari (a center for breeding
endangered species) in 1982-83. Deaths were recorded in Ireland,
Texas and San Diego as well. Laurie Marker, curator of cheetahs
at Wildlife Safari (which has one of the world's largest collections)
found that 29 percent of cheetah cubs die within six months and
only half ever reach adulthood.

By 1986, zoo veterinarians in this country become alarmed
over the poor fertility of captive cheetahs. Only 9-12 percent of
the sexually mature cheetahs in North American zoos produced
live cubs during 1981-86, compared with 60-80 percent in South
Africa.

Dietary culprit

In 1926 it was discovered that some plants possess estrogenic
substances. By 1975, more than 300 plants were reported to have
estrogenic activity. Estrogens can increase the size of the uterus,
causing it to become fibrous, and affect the liver. A 1946 report
by the Department of Agriculture in Western Australia high-
lighted the potential deleterious and widespread influence of plant
estrogens on animal reproduction. The fertility of sheep, grazing
on a subterranean strain of clover, declined progressively between
1941 to 1944. This infertility syndrome in sheep eventually
became known as "clover disease."

In 1984, Kenneth Setchell (along with some Swedish scientists) analyzed soybeans. A single meal of soy protein caused a
100- to 1000-fold increase in urinary estrogens, a significant biological factor. In 1986, Dr. Setchell suspected that the zoo diet
was responsible for cheetah sterility as well as an observed liver
pathology. At that time cheetahs in the Cincinnati Zoo were fed a

commercially prepared feline diet containing horse meat and by-products, soybeans, bone meal, liver, fish meal and vitamins and minerals. Soy protein made up between 5-13 percent of the diet.

Dr. Setchell's research team suggested changing the diet to a chicken based formulation containing no soy products. One animal in Cincinnati, a four-year-old who had never been pregnant, came into estrous three months after the zoo changed her diet. She mated and showed all the early signs of pregnancy, but unfortunately did not give birth. Removing estrogens from the diet doesn't always result in damage being repaired.

Concerned, after discovering the consequences of soy in the feline diet, we called Dr. Setchell and gave him technical data for our diets. He suspected that the amount of soy used in the soy containing *Vegecat* diets would have little effect on cats.

Soy derived daidzein and genistein contained in our diets is not higher than that of commercial diets used successfully by breeders. Domestic cats are notoriously fertile and infertility of dogs and cats is rare, even if fed a high proportion of soy protein.

Tofu possesses less estrogenic activity than most other soy products, as the following shows (contents in parts per million):

Phytoestrogen Content of Soy Products

PRODUCT	GENISTIN	DAIDZIN
Soybeans	747	117
Toasted, defatted flakes	1601	200
Textured soy protein	882	86
Breakfast patties	37	1
Soy sprouts (5 days)	403	92
Tofu	75	35
Soy sauce	0	0

Chapter 12

HEALTH &

HEALING

O ur primary goal in 1985, when we started our research, was to break the slaughterhouse link for vegetarian pet owners. We had hoped that vegetarian pets would *at least* be as healthy as those fed slaughterhouse products. Along the way we had a pleasant surprise: vegetarian pets are healthier. In retrospect we should have anticipated it. Pure and natural ingredients are so different from those found in commercial diets.

Living wild in nature, feral cats subsist mostly on mice with the occasional squirrel, chipmunk, rabbit or bird. It's a dangerous world out there and death usually results from other predators (especially while young), from eating poisoned animals, or ingesting man-made toxic materials while scavenging around wastes. This is in sharp contrast from those who share our homes, as the following chart reveals:

Leading Causes of Death

CATS	DOGS
1 Feline Leukemia	Cancer
2 Kidney disease/failure	Kidney Disease
3 Cancer	Old Age
4 Old Age	Heart Problems
5 Feline infectious peritonitis	Bloat
6 Heart Failure	Liver Problems

Sixteen-year-old rejuvenated

I visited northern Idaho in late 1990, staying with a lawyer friend who lived with two cats, Fritzie and Pasha. Pasha was an immense cat, about six years old weighing in at 16 pounds with bulky fur that made him look even bigger. He had very definite tastes, eating only cat kibble, according to his caretaker, Michael.

Fritzie was the elderly grand dame of the huge house. Delicate, feeble and skinny she looked all of her 16 years, and had been with Michael all of that time.

She was no longer able to make it to the numerous cat boxes around the house and so, as the resident cat expert, I soon found myself involved in following my nose and cleaning up the latest "accident." Her stools smelled *terrible*. At one point, a wayward stool under an end table inadvertently got sucked into an unlucky vacuum. The air in the entire house reeked with the stench! Frantic, we rushed to air out the house out before guests arrived.

You expect me to eat what?

Changing the animals' food became top priority. I put garbanzo vegetarian food into Fritzie's bowl, and she asked, in her cat way, "Do you really expect me to eat that?" and walked away. One-half hour later she checked her bowl to see if we had gotten the message. Nope, same stuff, but this time she gingerly nibbled it, and found it palatable enough to eat it all.

A few days later the entire household remarked about the amazing transformation of this feline "mother of all stenches." My job as chief cleaner-upper of litter boxes took a decided turn for the better. Fritzie still missed her cat box, but now I used my eyes, instead of nose, for finding her stools.

Michael could hardly get over the change. He pointed out to everybody the difference in her fur. For the first time in years it was soft, shining, and no longer felt greasy. Fritzie was so happy! People petted her so much she went around purring. The transformation seemed like a miracle.

Meanwhile, strong-minded Pasha observed these changes with concern. When we mixed the new food with the beloved kibble, he picked out the kibble. We were also strong-minded, and had the advantage of "good and right." Pasha just had pampered taste buds.

After nine days in the big house it was time to go back to Oregon. Pasha hadn't made the transition but nine days sometimes isn't long enough for a really stubborn and finicky cat, but the battle wasn't over.

Peer pressure

A month later, moving to Idaho, we continued Pasha's conversion. Now he had three vegetarian cats for examples, Fritzie (who had stayed vegetarian) and our two long time vegetarians, Veggie and Ebony.

It was too much for Pasha. In a couple of days Pasha gave in and started eating the same garbanzo recipe that everyone else ate and that was that!

A few weeks later Michael stopped practicing law, changed his life style by selling or giving away most of his possessions, and looked for new caretakers for his animals. Some folks adopted Fritzie, delighted with her matronly manner and health. The change in diet saved her from certain death at the pound.

Fritzie is not an isolated case. We've included accounts of other old cats (and dogs) acting young again. Why is this, and how can the "unnatural vegetarian diet" be superior to one based on flesh? Perhaps one reason is because there's a fundamental difference between food from plants and food from animals.

Metabolic wastes

Bodies of cows and coyotes, fish and fowl, and people and porcupines contain skeleton, muscle, nervous, circulatory, respiratory, gastrointestinal, metabolic (liver and hormonal), reproduction and excretion systems.

How well these systems function defines health. The excretory system includes the kidneys for ridding blood of unwanted substances such as the end-products of metabolic reactions. These ashes of the cellular fires would soon smother the flames themselves if not readily removed.

Meat-eaters poisoned by their diet

The ashes of urea, uric acid, creatinine, phenols, sulfates, and phosphates are poisons absent or negligible in plant life. Urea results from the splitting of amino acids, forming ammonia, which combines with carbon dioxide in the liver to produce urea. It is so toxic, especially to the brain, that too much leads to hepatic coma. Often, in that case, ammonia is found in the brain as well.

At the cellular level, purine, a basic building block of DNA, degrades in animal bodies to uric acid. An excess of uric acid causes aggressive behavior, arthritis, kidney stones, gout, and impaired kidney function leading to failure. Animal foods are much higher in purines than foods of vegetable origin.

These metabolic poisons are inescapable to flesh eaters. This is to say nothing of the additional manmade substances such as the estrogens and stilbesterol used to increase market size of animals. In addition there is a concentration of pesticides, fungicides, and heavy metal at the top of the food chain: animals.

With flesh consumption, the eliminatory system uses tremendous energy removing metabolic and other wastes. Cats and dogs, though well equipped to remove metabolic poisons, save energy if they don't have to contend with it at all. By eliminating meat from their diets, cat and dog bodies become rejuvenated by using energy that formerly eliminated ingested animal wastes.

*A*CUPUNCTURE

David Jaggar, introduced earlier, wrote in the *Vegepet Gazette:*

There are records that show that acupuncture has been used for over 3,000 years. The existence of acupuncture has been known in the West for about a century. However, it has only been introduced on a large scale over the past 15 years or so. Acupuncture is but one part of Traditional Chinese Medicine, which includes: herb therapy (the most often used), massage, therapeutic exercises, etc. It is estimated that one quarter of the world's population benefits from acupuncture as a major form of medical treatment.

Traditionally, acupuncture is practiced within the scope of a broad "philosophy of life" that is somewhat different from those that are dominant in the West. While there is no space to discuss these ideas here, traditional acupuncturists concern themselves with manipulating body energy to restore the energy balance of the body and in turn improve the body's various organ systems.

The Western approach tends to have a mechanistic viewpoint of life. So Western physicians see the human body as a complex machine, and they rely on surgery and drugs to fix this machine. However, there is no understanding of what makes someone alive! It is this "vital energy" that is central to the Oriental approach. This is not to say that Western medicine is not very valuable. It is, but mostly for dire, life-threatening situations. For routine health care, prevention, and treatment of chronic dis-eases, for which Western medicine has such limited success, the traditional Chinese medical approaches come to the fore.

Holistic medicine

Once I heard about acupuncture, I became intensely interested in the subject, because I had become disillusioned with so much of veterinary medicine as practiced in the West. Veterinarians were, and still are, working almost as technicians, routinely injecting antibiotics and steroids, and doing routine surgeries, waiting for less common cases to break the monotony. There is less and less contact with the animal and little appreciation for the unique character of any particular patient's health problem, such as dermatitis (inflammation of the skin). Questions such as, what is it about this particular animal that it expresses its unbalanced state of health in this particular way, are not usually considered in the West. Answers to these kinds of questions are important to the satisfactory treatment from an Oriental approach, and rather than just treating the symptoms of a disease, attempts are made to get to the deeper sources of health problems. Acupuncture, therefore, comes under the domain of holistic medicine.

Other than for a few selected treatments, acupuncture requires considerable knowledge and experience as well as an open mind to appreciate that the body is something more than the detailed anatomy and physiology as taught in the West. A few veterinary colleagues and I formed the International Veterinary Acupuncture Society (IVAS), in 1975. This has become the sole organization outside China and Japan representing and advancing veterinary acupuncture internationally and within the USA. IVAS organizes courses and other meetings to educate graduate veterinarians in this useful modality, which is not yet taught as part of the core curriculum in veterinary colleges.

IVAS promotes and encourages scientific investigation and research into the physiology and practice of veterinary acupuncture. We also incorporate what has been shown to be beneficial from human acupuncture research (much of which has been conducted on animals). As a result there is now a solid base of research to substantiate the effectiveness of acupuncture. In 1988, the American Veterinary Medical Association gave formal recognition to the practice of veterinary acupuncture.

Uses

By now, you are probably wondering what acupuncture can be used for. There are many indications. One of the main areas is for muscle and skeletal problems, and this aspect is frequently used to help horses. It has been shown to be useful for many problems in other systems of the body, such as for skin problems, certain neurologic problems (for example with certain disc diseases), respiratory problems, stomach and intestinal problems, and circulatory problems, shock, etc.

Acupuncture is not a panacea; it is not a "cure-all." However, in conditions where it is indicated, it has frequently yielded very satisfactory results. It is especially indicated wherever conventional Western medical therapies are unsuccessful or are contraindicated due to side effects, and where surgery is not feasible, and should be considered before more drastic measures are taken (except for life-threatening situations).

Methods

Veterinarians trained in acupuncture have studied the few hundred points to use for the various conditions and how to analyze an animal's health problem from an Oriental perspective. They may then elect to treat the animal using one of a variety of methods. These include the traditional use of acupuncture needles; stimulation of the points with very mild electric current; injection of the points; heating the points or treating points with a low intensity laser.

During treatment, particularly subsequent treatments, most animals are quite relaxed, rarely requiring any form of tranquilization. The number of treatments varies with the particular problem, with the more long standing diseases usually requiring more treatments. Usually two to three treatments are given per week, and an evaluation made after three or four treatments to plan the course of action from there. After initial beneficial response, treatments can cut back to once a week, or month, or every six months should the problem recur, or be discontinued altogether.

Veterinary acupuncture is an invaluable addition to the therapeutic methods available to veterinarians. It is especially helpful to geriatric pets as an approach to maintain their quality of life. While more research is needed, acupuncture is an exciting new field in Western veterinary medicine, and now that its benefits are widely recognized, its use is sure to grow in the years ahead.

For more information, write to the International Veterinary Acupuncture Society listed in Resources.

ARTHRITIS

Michael Lemmon permitted us to print his recommendations for arthritis:

Free radicals

What are free radicals? They sound dangerous, and they are. You may have read about them recently in connection with the aging process and with degenerative diseases. How are they formed? What kind of damage do they do? Most importantly, how does the body protect itself against them?

One of the contributing causes of arthritis is the excess accumulation of free radicals in the joint capsule — the fluid-filled sac surrounding every joint in the body.

This fluid, or "joint oil" is kept healthy with the help of enzymes produced by the body. The enzymes act like soap, they clean away the free radicals, keeping the joint properly lubricated and allowing free movement. Otherwise, the free radicals would slowly eat away the lining of the joint capsule, causing pain and swelling.

Those with arthritic animals know the stiff, painful legacy of this disease, as joints get seemingly "frozen" into position.

What can be done about this? First, it helps to know where free radicals come from.

Free radicals are formed during normal cellular metabolism, when cells take in nutrients, assimilate and utilize the nutrients, and then excrete the waste products.

Some of these waste products are free radicals. Wherever you find poor quality foods being eaten, you will also find an excess of free radicals.

Rancid fats and moldy grains are two leading sources of free radical production in animals. Where do they come from?

Commercial pet foods.

Fat is an essential ingredient in any diet. Many commercial pet food manufacturers have problems with controlling the rancidity in fats added to the food they produce. They unsuccessfully use chemicals to try to curb this rancidity.

American grain is quite often polluted with varying degrees of mold. Pet food manufacturers, for economic reasons, usually use the lower quality grain products in their pet food.

Chemicals and pollutants in our air, water, and food supply also significantly increase free radical production.

Free radicals, if they are not neutralized by antioxidants, will cause damage to the body's tissue systems, as the example of arthritis below demonstrates.

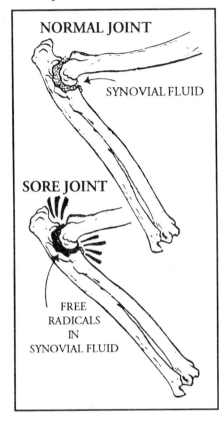

NORMAL JOINT

SYNOVIAL FLUID

SORE JOINT

FREE RADICALS IN SYNOVIAL FLUID

There is, however, protection. Many cases of arthritis will respond effectively and quickly to antioxidant nutrients such as vitamin C, vitamin E, beta-carotene, and selenium.

The daily amounts vary with the size of the pet. Smaller pets (10 to 25 pounds) could use 500 to 1,000 mg of vitamin C, 200 to 400 units of vitamin E, and 50 to 100 mcgm of selenium.

For the best protection, it is good to prepare homemade meals for your pets in order to avoid the rancid fats, moldy grains, and chemicals that are present in most commercial foods.

Since many pet owners rely on the convenience of commercial foods, however, it becomes doubly important to supplement your pet's diet with antioxidants.

S.O.D. — catalase enzymes

Another highly effective antioxidant is the enzyme combination of superoxide dismutase (S.O.D.) and catalase.

These two enzymes are produced in the cells of our bodies. We are each born with an enzyme "bank." Babies have twice as much S.O.D. — catalase as adults. These

S.O.D. — catalase enzymes are the most effective free radical destroyers. They also help remove other poisons and toxins.

The body's ability to produce S.O.D. — catalase decreases with age. There is good evidence that over time, the excessive use of the body's enzyme system also decreases this enzyme production. Sparing the body's enzyme "bank," or reserve, by consuming raw foods that are rich in enzymes (or by taking enzyme supplements), helps solve this free radical problem.

Another solution is to take S.O.D. — catalase supplements. They are derived from wheat sprouts. It takes a large amount of sprouts to make one tablet — that contains more than one million units of S.O.D. — catalase!

These supplements have proven very helpful for arthritis and other geriatric degenerative problems in my practice as well as in the practice of other veterinarians throughout the country. S.O.D. — catalase supplements are harmless.

The amount given depends on the size of the pet and also on the severity of the condition. Sometimes a higher amount of six to ten pills and even more are given daily to more quickly reduce the buildup of free radicals and other toxins in the body. This reduces the pain and inflammation of the condition, allowing the veterinarian to prescribe lower doses as needed.

Rather than treat arthritis and other degenerative problems in the older pet with heavy doses of steroids and other drugs — which may have harmful side effects — we can instead rely on the use of these simple, effective antioxidants that work in harmony with the body, assisting it in its daily routine, helping it to alleviate pain, discomfort, and disease.

Information about S.O.D. — catalase supplements may be obtained from Biotec Foods-Biovet International.

BLOAT

Affecting 40-60,000 dogs each year in the United States, bloat is the fifth leading cause of death, annually killing up to 36,000. Middle-aged and older, deep-chested large breeds of dogs such as Danes, St. Bernards, and bloodhounds are most susceptible, although it sometimes strikes small dogs and even cats.

Bloat is an incredibly fast acting ailment, in which a perfectly healthy dog (rarely cat) dies three hours after a meal. The stomach distends like a balloon, and the skin about the stomach is so taut from expansion that it sounds like a drum when snapped with a finger. Death comes from gas pressure against the heart and lungs.

Factors that increase the possibility for bloat include large meals fed in a single feeding, exercising immediately after eating, excessive dietary calcium, bolting the food, and excessive excitement during mealtime. Veterinarian Leon Whitney stated that all of his losses to bloat occurred during the night. He feeds his main meal to his dogs in the morning because of his experience.

The consensus of evidence states that a cereal based diet is not a contributing factor.

To eliminate this risk, feed your animal at least two meals a day, in a quiet environment, and not late at night.

FLEAS

When Veggie first came to us as a stray, fleas covered most of his body, although he seemed well fed. We switched him to the vegetarian diet (he had no choice). At first the fleas were so bad that my youngest son got quite adept at running his narrow fingers through Veggie's fur and finding fleas. Veggie's ears sometimes were a mass of them. This took place every day, removing some 10-20 fleas.

Not trusting commercial products such as nerve gas flea collars and insecticides, we tried the usual home remedies such as oils of eucalyptus, rosemary, and pennyroyal. Maybe they had some effect, but it was hard to see any difference. We didn't know then about spraying him with water that had soaked a raw lemon peel overnight.

Nutritional yeast

We kept feeding him vegetarian fare, which included a good amount of nutritional yeast, every day. Yeast is loaded in B vitamins. After a few months, we saw a substantial difference in his infestation. Finally, there were no more fleas.

This past summer has been one of the warmest on record. In late spring a story in the local newspaper warned pet owners that fleas and ticks were expected in record numbers. Yet this entire season, just as in the last couple of years, Veggie has had *no* fleas, and neither has his spirited companion cat, Ebony.

Thiamin

Of the more than 20 B vitamins, thiamin seems the one most effective in building flea resistance. Thiamin is more energetic with the entire B complex, rather than used alone.

Ola Donadio, writing in *Repel Fleas Nutritionally,* tells the story of one veterinarian who gave his dog 200mg thiamin daily. Soon the dog had no fleas, but by the fourth week the infestation returned worse than ever. Donadio theorizes that this was because it isn't possible to supply thiamin in such large doses without upsetting the balance of other B vitamins.

Yeast has a well-deserved grass roots reputation for boosting an animal's immunity to fleas, but its effects are evident only after prolonged use. Because there isn't much profit in testing nutritional yeast, the few research projects that involved this "folk remedy" were short-lived.

One 1983 study, published in the *Journal of the American Veterinary Medical Association,* found no difference between dogs fed 14 grams of brewer's yeast per day and controls fed none. The study concluded after five weeks, finding yeast ineffective for controlling fleas.

Another study, published in the *Journal of the American Animal Hospital Association,* came to the same conclusion. Fed 100mg thiamin twice daily, dogs still had fleas after *two* weeks and the study was discontinued.

These short term studies provide *proof* to some allopathic veterinarians that yeast, or more specifically, thiamin, provide no flea control, leaving intact the profits from powerful commercial products.

Garlic bouquet

While some people swear *at* garlic, others swear *by* garlic. It has a wide range of documented benefits, including strengthening the immune system. Pat Johnson, writing in *Cat Love,* says:

> Raw garlic is a wonderful flea repellent because it makes the cat's blood unappealing to parasites. Crush a little garlic in your cat's meal everyday while you're fighting fleas. For cats not under siege by fleas, you can add garlic twice a week to the diet to make sure fleas don't even attempt to dine at your cat's expense. I know some people don't believe that garlic works, but I've seen it do wonders.

For fleas, try giving a part or all of a low potency B complex vitamin every day, until there are no more fleas.

FUS

FUS (feline urologic syndrome) is the second biggest killer of cats. Estimates of the percentage of cats susceptible to FUS varies from one to more than 13 percent. Work with your vet if you suspect FUS, since it is life threatening.

Studies indicate that FUS affects more females than males, although males are more prone to blockage. There is no difference between intact and neutered cats. The first episode occurs usually between the ages of one and three, with more than 80 percent occurring in the first six years of age.

Symptoms

Difficult urination, squatting, voiding tiny amounts of urine, blood in the urine, and excess licking of genitalia are symptomatic of FUS. In about 30 percent of the cases, a secondary infection (usually staphylococcus) of the urinary tract complicates recovery. If not immediately taken care of, FUS can lead to complete obstruction of the urinary tract resulting in vomiting, depression, dehydration, coma, convulsions, and death.

Complete obstruction must be removed, either by massage, flushing, or in severe cases by surgery. As a last resort vets can puncture the bladder with a hypodermic needle and draw out the urine. It may be necessary to stabilize visibly dehydrated cats by giving fluids by an intravenous catheter.

CAUSE

Domestic cats are thought to have evolved from small desert cats. Often their only water intake consisted of the liquid found in their prey's bodies, thus they formed a more concentrated urine than other animals. This concentrated solution can form minute stones or crystals (uroliths) that irritate the lining of the urinary tract (cystitis), and may completely obstruct the urethra.

Studies point to two major factors contributing to FUS: a high concentration of urolith forming constituents and an alkaline urine.

Magnesium

It is not the dietary ash of the food that is important as much as the magnesium content. Ash consists of all non-combustible materials, such as mineral salts. A diet relatively high in ash may have a high phosphorus content and at the same time be low in magnesium, thus preventing FUS.

Studies from 1971-82 indicated that 90-97 percent of all uraliths are struvite, a calculus composed of magnesium and ammonium phosphate bonded with water. By 1986 this figure had dropped to 82 percent, primarily because of more acidic diets containing less magnesium. Other uraliths may consist of calcium oxalate, calcium phosphate, and ammonium urate (uric acid).

Commercial cat foods (both dry and canned) contain on the average .16 percent magnesium on a dry basis. Some (such as *Puss 'N Boots Fish*) contain as much as .29 percent. One of the lowest, sold primarily by veterinarians, is Hill's *Prescription Diet Feline s/d* containing .06 percent (.058 percent for canned and .055 percent for dry) magnesium. Hill's does *not* recommend it for maintenance, but specifically for struvite urolith dissolution.

Hill's *Prescription Diet c/d,* sold as a very low magnesium diet for cats who have had occurrences of FUS in the past and to prevent new occurrences from happening to cats without a history of FUS, contains .07 percent magnesium, the same as HOANA's *Vegecat* diet *Glorious Gluten*. In a study involving rats, dietary magnesium of .07 percent completely dissolved struvite calculi in four weeks, whereas calculi doubled in size at .27 percent.

In spite of this and other documentation, Joan Harper advises adding more dietary magnesium for FUS, stating, "If you are not giving a magnesium supplement (see chapter on supplements) start using one, and if you are increase it." She gives cats an additional 100mg magnesium per day, besides the 50mg from their food. It is difficult to determine the rational for this, yet Harper has quite a following. Her 1992 book, *The Healthy Cat and Dog Cook Book*, is in its seventh edition (the first was in 1975).

Ingredient choices

Since overwhelming evidence indicts magnesium, choose lower magnesium ingredients for home recipes. If you use tofu (a good form of soy), obtain tofu coagulated with nigariko (calcium sulfate) instead of nigari (magnesium chloride). When using grains, stay away from whole grains since minerals are concentrated in seed coats.

Cats require high dietary protein and phosphorus relative to magnesium, therefore cat urine usually contains enough ammonium and phosphate for struvite formation *if* sufficient magnesium is present. The critical mass depends upon one more factor — the pH (acidity or alkalinity) of the urine.

Acid urine

Struvite forms best in alkaline urine. Cystine and urate calculi form best in *acid* urine, but these constitute less than three percent of all uroliths. Urine pH has no effect on infrequent oxalate and calcium phosphate uroliths.

Anitra Frazier says the mere *smell* of food causes body chemistry turn urine alkaline. This is one reason she gives for not leaving food down all day long. However, urine pH is unpredictable on that basis, according to research conducted at Mark Morris Associates in Kansas. Some foods fed free choice (rather than at intervals) made urine more alkaline. Other foods fed the same way turned urine more acid. By changing from free choice to interval feeding, foods flipped sides, some turning urine acid and others turning it alkaline.

We agree it's best to keep feeding areas clean, feeding fresh food in clean surroundings and removing leftovers in a reasonable amount of time.

Bathtub laboratory

One of our acquaintances tests his vegetarian cat's urine almost every day, concerned from his past experience with FUS. This way he knows the influence of specific specific foods on urine, guiding him to those more acid. We wondered how he conveniently checked the urine, and he replied that his cat used the *bathtub* for a litter box, making it easy for him to test urine with litmus (a paper coated with certain lichens that turns shades of red or blue — indicating the degree of acidity or alkalinity). He wets the litmus paper in fresh urine and then checks its color with a calibrated, colored legend.

Another method (however more expensive) involves a special litter that changes color. Your vet may know about this.

A question of balance

Metabolism does not oxidize mineral elements in foods. Residue (ash) that remains is either acid or alkaline. By changing the composition of the diet, urine pH changes one way or the other.

The lungs and the kidneys dispose of acid end products of food metabolism. Lungs remove carbon dioxide. Kidneys remove hydrogen ions from the body and at the same time return bicarbonate to the blood, helping maintain blood pH within narrow limits. Items not acid in taste, such as cereals, meat, eggs, and bread, become strongly acid when their end products reach the blood and urine, since most protein foods (and most seeds) contain a preponderance of acid forming elements such as sulfur, phosphorus, and chlorine. Their metabolism yield sulfuric and phosphoric acids, *increasing* urine acidity.

Conversely, organic acids of fruits and vegetables, when oxidized, become carbon dioxide, water and a residue of potassium, calcium, sodium and magnesium, turning urine more alkaline.

A matter of choice

Abridged from *Acid & Alkaline* (Herman Aihara), the following shows how foods change urine pH. Numbers indicate milliliters of a known solution that neutralized the original ash solution.

Acid & Alkaline Foods

ACID FORMING		ALKALINE FORMING	
Egg Yolk	19.2	Kidney beans	18.8
Oatmeal	17.8	Spinach	15.6
Brown rice	15.5	Soybeans	10.2
Tuna	15.3	Bananas	8.8
Chicken	10.4	Azuki beans	7.3
Horse meat	6.6	Carrots	6.4
Peanuts	5.4	Potatoes	5.4
Beef	5.0	Cabbage	4.9
Fava beans	4.4	Sweet potatoes	4.3
Cheese	4.3	Apples	3.4
Peas	2.5	Watermelon	2.1
Bread	0.6	String beans	1.1
Asparagus	0.1	Tofu	0.1

Testing the reaction of food ashes (duplicating digestion) with an acid (or alkaline) solution of known strength until it tests neutral (a process called titration), determines pH. This shows how specific foods influence the acidity, alkalinity, or neutrality of body fluids, including urine. Kidneys maintain the blood pH within narrow limits by excreting excess acid or alkali in the urine.

Time travel

Considering the long evolutionary adaptation of felines to (acid forming) meat, a proper dietary approach must emphasize *non*-alkaline foods. How long have cats consumed prey?

Egypt tamed cats 5,000 years ago, but paleontologists trace cats all the way to the Paleocene epoch, 65 million years ago, pointing to a small carnivorous mammal called the creodont.

Forerunners of the Cat

Years Ago	Epoch	Name	Description
65M	Paleocene	Creodont	Carnivorous mammal
54M	Eocene	Miacid	Carnivorous mammal
38M	Oligocene	Dinictis	Stabbing cat
26M	Miocene	Pseudaelurus	Stabbing cat
7M	Pliocene	Felis lunensis	Biting cat
2.5M	Pleistocene	Felidae	Modern cat

The Pleistocene Period saw a world filled with lions, lynx, giant cheetahs, leopards, jaguars, and smaller felines such as the manul (still extant) and Martelli's wild cat. A million years ago, saber-tooth cats roamed Europe, Asia and the Americas, killing thick-skinned elephants and rhinos. The last of these cats became extinct 14,500 years ago. From Martelli's wild cat, about 600,000 years ago, felis silvestris spread over Europe, Asia and Africa. Today's domestic cat *(Felis domesticus)* is probably the direct descendent of the African version *(F. lybica)*.

Flesh-eaters for ages, cats evolved totally different nutrient needs from humans. Since the metabolic residue of flesh is acid, cats developed a finely tuned physiology that handles acid residue well, but at the same time losing the adaptability to preponderantly alkaline foods chosen by in omnivorous and other animals.

At variance with this, Anitra Frazier erroneously states in *It's A Cat's Life,* that all-meat diets (for cats) promote an *alkaline* urine. She also says, "I frequently recommend including alkalizing vegetables in a cat's food... ...while the veterinarian treats the disease, you can use foods to alkalize the cat's system." This is fine advice for a sick human, but not for a cat. Frazier avoids feeding tomato and potato because "they tend to produce an acid condition...," but research in 1978 found three different brands of tomato juice elevated urine pH (made it more alkaline).

Acid forming plant foods

Fortunately, the main vegetarian foods we advocate feeding are acid forming. Asparagus, peas, brown rice, and oats are all acid foods. Omitted by Aihara, but on other lists of acid forming foods are: lentils, garbanzos, corn, Brussels sprouts, lamb's-quarters, most nuts (except almonds and coconut) and grains (not millet). Wheat gluten is also a relatively strong acid residue food.

Choosing acid producing foods along with low dietary magnesium intake alleviates conditions that create FUS.

DRY FOODS

Several studies suggest that feeding dry commercial pet foods contributes to the growing incidence of FUS, even though, as mentioned previously, dry and canned foods contain the same average percentage of magnesium on a dry weight basis. In this country, one study found that FUS increased 1.7 times when a regular commercial dry food made up 50-75 percent of the diet, 3.1 times for 75-99 percent of the diet, and increased 6.7 times if fed exclusively. A similar Dutch study found cats fed dry food experiencing seven times more FUS than if a dry food was never fed.

Another study found urinary magnesium concentration three times greater when cats consumed dry food, even though the canned diet contained the *same* dry weight percentage of magnesium. Examining foods for units of magnesium per dietary calories of metabolizable energy helps explain this seeming anomaly.

Magnesium/dietary energy density

Since the caloric density of dry food is less than for other forms of food, cats eat more of it for energy needs — about 20 percent more and that means more magnesium.

Hill's *Prescription Diet Feline s/d* contains 11mg/100kcalME (per 100 calories of metabolizable energy). *Vegecat Glorious Gluten* contains 15mg/100kcalME. Except for the Hill's *s/d* just mentioned, the 15mg figure compares favorably with the lowest amounts for *any* commercial food. For example, *Prescription Diet c/d* (Hill's) is the next lowest, and has the identical 15mg figure, along with the same .07 percent dietary magnesium.

Compare these figures with that of the largest selling dry cat food in the world, *Cat Chow*. Ralston Purina's flagship kibble contains an amazing 43mg/100kcalME (.16 percent magnesium on a dry weight basis). That pales in comparison to *Puss 'N Boots Tuna* weighing in at 84mg/100kcalME (.25 percent mg/DW)!

More concentrated urine

Dry cat foods probably contribute to FUS in another, unrelated way. Food ingested in the form of biscuits or kibble creates a demand for water, but even if enough water is drunk to equal that which would have been in a canned or home prepared food, one study found more water excreted in the feces. That leaves less water available for diluting the urine.

Most commercial dry foods contain more fiber, are less digestible, and have less caloric density than do canned foods. These factors increase magnesium concentration and set up the conditions leading to FUS.

Stress

Anitra Frazier states "It's a generally accepted fact that feline urologic syndrome, although caused by an alkaline condition in the urine, is emotionally triggered."

I'm not able to verify this since the scientific literature on FUS doesn't mention stress as a factor. Stress plays an undeniably major role in human health, and by analogy it makes sense to eliminate stress for sick animals. Many influences create stress, such as a noisy household, the pet caretaker's own emotional state, changes in the environment, strangers, chemical irritants (flea collars, smoke and deodorizers), drafts and extreme heat or cold.

A warm, cuddly environment goes a long way towards recovery in any illness, for people *and* pets.

Our vegetarian cat had FUS

Our three-year-old developed FUS after eating the oats with soy (textured vegetable protein) diet for about a year. We switched Priya to the lentil recipe, and gave her vitamin C. All symptoms left within a week and then we changed her diet once more, to the garbanzo recipe, which she found more tasty, and FUS never bothered her again. We detected the ailment early and it wasn't necessary to add additional vitamins to her diet. If she had been slower to recover we could have fed her the wheat gluten recipe, as well as additional vitamins. Remember, FUS is life threatening. Veterinarians are life savers in critical times and have the expertise to know what emergency procedures may be necessary.

Richard Pitcairn suggests initiating treatment with an easier to digest diet, such as a broth made from potatoes, squash, broccoli, and soy sauce along with meat or bones. We would leave out the meat or bones. Cats like cooked squash and this easy to digest vegetable will relieve eliminatory organs of some of their burden. Afterwards change to a lower magnesium diet.

Water consumption

Make sure plenty of *fresh* water is readily available. Urine is a mixture of different substances in solution and the more concentrated urine is, the faster stones form. Adding additional salt, or salty foods makes cats drink more, which thins urine.

Vitamin C and E

Add vitamin C (ascorbic acid) to the diet. Pulverize tablets or use ascorbic acid powder, which is commonly available. For a 10-pound cat we recommend as much as 2000mg per day. This amount reduces urine pH, but may not be enough to dissolve struvite uroliths.

Don't use buffered forms of vitamin C since part of the reason for using vitamin C is to make urine more acid. Since vitamin C is effective on infection, it helps some cases of FUS on that level as well. For long term maintenance, we recommend as much as 1000mg per day. If other urine acidifiers are used, use only 500mg.

Adding a minimum of 60 IU and up to 300 IU of Vitamin E per day helps irritated tissues heal with minimum or no scarring.

Methionine

Low quality commercial diets may be low on methionine, which may contribute to alkaline urine. All the *Vegecat* diets contain adequate amounts of methionine, in line with recommendations of the Natural Research Council.

As an end-product of methionine's metabolism, sulfuric acid excreted into urine makes it more acid. In addition, sulfate displaces phosphate from magnesium-ammonium-phosphate, i.e., struvite. These two factors prove significant for dissolving struvites and preventing new ones from forming.

Methionine, a natural amino acid in protein (although found sometimes in inadequate amounts), can be added to the diet with *relative* safety. Adding too much reduces urine pH to dangerous levels (less than 5.9), inducing metabolic acidosis. Excessively acidic urine may, in time, lead to osteoporosis (loss of bone calcium), and potassium and electrolyte imbalances affecting neurological and muscular performances. Methionine (as well as ammonium chloride) in amounts safe for mature cats have proved toxic for kittens, decreasing growth and if fed in larger amounts, can be fatal.

A conservative amount to add for struvite dissolution is 1,000mg methionine per day (for a 10-pound cat) taken *with* meals. This maintains urine acidity at between 6.1 to 6.2 and is under the estimated 1,800mg upper limit. Add it during food preparation.

Is nutritional yeast a factor?

Some people worry about the possibility of nutritional yeast contributing to urinary tract blockages.

Ammonium urate or uric acid crystals affect 22 out of every 10,000 cats. Chances that your cat has this kind of urolith is rare.

If, after two weeks, signs of FUS are still evident after feeding an acid forming, low magnesium diet, consider the possibly of infection or the presence of a non-struvite urolith.

Urinary urate concentration increases with increased ingestion of purines. Foods of animal origin contain the most purines, such as muscle tissue with about .1 percent purine content. Other animal tissues contain amounts up to one percent, such as certain fish, as well as the hearts, livers, and brains of animals.

Nutritional yeast contains seven to eight percent nucleic acids. Ninety percent are RNA and 10 percent are DNA. Nineteen percent of the nucleotide base in DNA is guanine; 31 percent is adenine. Both of these bases are purine derivatives, therefore the purine content of nutritional yeast is about .4 percent.

The amount of nutritional yeast used in our recipes is low compared to the bulk of the other ingredients. An animal on a meat based diet ingests more purines.

Add a low potency vitamin B complex tablet to a week's worth of food if nutritional yeast is omitted from our recipes.

Healing herbs

Richard Pitcairn recommends equisetum arvense (horsetail grass). Steep two teaspoons of the dried herb in one-half cup of hot water. Give one-fourth teaspoon of this infusion three times a day for a week or two, let up a week, and repeat if needed.

Since cats with FUS may feel cold, the herb stinging nettle has had good results in making the cat feel warm and it helps tame bladder spasm. Use either in the homeopathic 3x preparation or as the dried herb, giving a small tablet every two hours for four treatments, then one tablet every six hours for four treatments, followed by one tablet every eight hours, and one tablet daily for a few weeks.

HEART PROBLEMS

Vitamin E is an important vitamin to treat cardiac problems. In active cases we advise gradually working up to 400 IU every third day for cats. For dogs, Dr. Belfield recommends 100 IU for small, 200 IU for medium and larger, and 400 IU per day for giant breeds.

If you add vitamin C, avoid sodium ascorbate, as well as all sodium compounds. Cut back on salt by giving just one-half of the amount called for in the recipes.

Juliette de Bairacli Levy has success in treating heart disease with strong rosemary tea along with honey. She says that rosemary is a tonic, a cleanser, and a nervine, all desirable in this treatment. She also recommends dandelion and watercress leaves.

How to Have A Healthier Dog, and *The Very Healthy Cat Book* by Belfield and Zucker detail vitamin thearapy and *Dr. Pitcairn's Complete Guide to Natural Health for Dogs & Cats* gives extensive homeopathic recommendations.

HOMEOPATHY

Michael Lemmon, a strong advocate of homeopathy, writes:
Many conditions that plague your pet could be solved simply by using homeopathy. These helpful and harmless remedies are preferable to drugs. For those interested in this form of healing, I recommend adding the following two books to your library.

British veterinarian George MacLeod has written books on how to use homeopathic remedies on cattle, horses, and dogs. In the *Homeopathic Treatment of Dogs* MacLeod writes about each body system and then describes briefly some of the disease conditions in that system, telling which remedies would be helpful. For example, under the urinary system he lists interstitial nephritis (kidney inflammation), pyelonephritis, nephrosis, urolithiasis (stones in the urinary tract) and cystitis (bladder inflammation). He briefly describes the disease, including clinical signs, then lists four to thirteen remedies that may help each condition.

There is a good index in the back of the book to help find diseases quickly. His books on cattle and horses follow a similar format.

A section on virus diseases such as parvo and distemper gives helpful information on an alternative to vaccination: nosodes, which are homeopathic remedies made from diseased tissues or discharges. He describes experiments that demonstrate their safety and their high levels of protection.

Another British veterinarian, Christopher Day, has authored *The Homeopathic Treatment of Small Animals*. This book has a chapter describing homeopathic history and philosophy; it tells how homeopathy works. The same chapter also offers a rational defense against some of the common criticisms of homeopathy.

Other chapters advise the lay person when to consult a veterinarian. The pet owner should be able to find many good suggestions on how to use specific homeopathic remedies for specific conditions, such as simple digestive upsets, stiffness in the legs, and psychological problem.

For the veterinarian, there is a chapter on how to take the history in preparation for deciding upon a remedy. There is good information on how to manage the case, what potency to use, and how frequently to use the remedy.

There is also a good section on suggested remedies for disease conditions. One example is entropion, an inversion of the eyelid margin causing irritation to the eye, which occurs in some boxers, chows and great Danes. Day recommends *Borax* to alleviate the condition and, perhaps, thereby avoid surgery. I have seen several cases where this has proven true using *Borax 6X* twice daily.

Another condition mentioned is joint pain and stiffness, which is worse just after resting and gets better by moving around and exercising. The classical remedy here is *Rhus tox* and I have seen this work successfully many times. There is also a small section covering diseases in rabbits, guinea pigs, hamsters, rats, mice, and birds.

Disease prevention, including the use of nosodes in preventing infectious diseases, are also discussed. He writes of using *Caulophyllum* for birthing.

There are many other helpful sections telling about current research in veterinary homeopathy, a bibliography, plus a good index.

Both these authors offer valuable guidance and considerable information to assist veterinarians and pet owners interested in veterinary homeopathy.

The above books are available through Homeopathic Educational Services (see Resources).

VACCINATION

Six hundred readers responded to a recent *Cat Fancy* magazine poll on health. Four percent of the cats in the survey experienced adverse reactions to vaccines, most occurring after inoculation against feline leukemia. Mild reactions included mild lethargy and muscle soreness. More rare was foaming at the mouth, high temperature, vomiting, loss of bodily functions and seizure.

Each year billions of doses of vaccines are administered to domestic animals. Live and modified-live agent vaccines induce the strongest reactions since they reproduce in the host.

Origin of vaccines

Of concern to ethical vegetarians, who refrain from using slaughterhouse products, is the origin of vaccines.

Passing rabies virus (as it occurs in nature) from brain to brain of rabbits results in a "fixed" virus. By injecting this virus into rabbit (and other animal) brains, a source of rabid animals is available. The rabid animals exhibit depraved appetite, pain at the site of inoculation, extreme sensitivity to noise and drafts, foaming at the mouth, inability to swallow, inability to find a comfortable position, tremors and convulsions. A massive convulsive seizure, or cardiac or respiratory failure would end their torture, but they are are killed in the last stages of the disease. Their brains, with accompanying spinal cords, form the basis for rabies vaccine, which contains 20 percent brain tissue suspended in a .5 percent solution of phenol. For vaccination, dogs typically get a dose of one cubic centimeter.

Recommendations

Richard Pitcairn cautiously endorses *some* vaccinations. Due to many adverse effects and sometimes limited protection, he says it isn't necessary to vaccinate for everything. For dogs he recommends (in his 1982 book): rabies, distemper and hepatitis, and perhaps parvovirus (for those exposed to large numbers of possibly ill animals) vaccines. For cats his only recommendation is for distemper.

The second leading infectious killer of cats, feline infectious peritonitis (FIP), now has vaccine available given like nose drops.

How much exposure your animal has to other animals and yards may affect your decision to vaccinate. If you decide to vaccinate, holistic veterinarians recommend singular vaccinations, since multiple ones may confuse the immune system.

As an alternative to vaccines, consider nosodes. These are homeopathic preparations taken gradually, boosting the body's immune response to a particular disease.

Appendix 1

COMMERCIAL PET FOODS

From New York, Karen Kozlow wrote:

I knew commercial food was bad when my dog, Epoo, developed cancer and heart trouble. The vet said to switch to a natural dog food, so I tried Cornucopia from the health food store, but because there were no preservatives, a lot of the times I would buy a bag that had developed maggots in it, so I said "forget it!" and just cooked her vegetables instead.

...Now Epoo has since passed away, and my dog, Misha, has been raised on a mostly vegetarian diet. She'll be three years old in August, and still has the "puppy" in her. I am thrilled to know that you have a supplement for my dog's food that will help me convince my family and friends that I am not harming my dog.

Once in a while they would make me feel guilty, but just looking at Misha's shiny black fur and her bounce of energy convinced me I wasn't a terrible "mother!"

Karen found that commercial pet food companies often make unsubstantiated claims. It's not enough just to *sustain* life — it's the *quality* of life that is important.

Prior to commercial foods, which wasn't *that* long ago, dogs and cats ate table scraps (consisting mostly of flesh). *The Dog in Health and Disease* (1872) stated:

The food of hounds is composed of meal flavored with broth to which more or less flesh is added, or with scraps as a substitute when flesh cannot be obtained.

After boiling the flesh until the meat readily leaves the bones, take all out with a pitchfork and put it to cool, skim all the fat off the broth and fill up with water.

Next mix the meal carefully with cold water and then pour this into the hot broth. Boil gently until it has been on the fire for half an hour. Draw the fire and ladle out the stuff into the coolers where it remains until it has set with the solidity of puddings.

Once a week some green food or potatoes or turnips should be boiled with the puddings.

As this was inconvenient, it was just a matter of time before someone applied the same commercial food skills that developed hardtack for feeding soldiers (fighting in the American Revolutionary War) to feeding dogs.

Commercial dog biscuits

In the year 1860, James Spratt, a lightning rod salesman, offered his dog some hard, stale, ship biscuits. His hungry dog woofed them down. Thinking he might have a bigger market for "dog biscuits" than for lightning rods, he set to work.

The first biscuits, baked on huge cookie sheets, contained mostly cereal products. By scoring the dough, biscuits conveniently broke, but crumbling them further made them absorb water or other liquids quicker and they become more palatable to dogs. Before long, flesh mixed with the dough ushered in a new age of convenience, ensuring the success of *Meat Fibrine* dog food. It was introduced with a full color display billboard, the first on a London store, picturing American Indians providing meat for the new product by killing bison.

Competion by the 1930s resulted in over 200 brands of canned dog food sitting on dealer shelves. Knowing little about nutritional requirements, processors sometimes sold the same exact contents as cat or dog food, by using different labels.

Before World War II, canned food constituted 91percent of the market. With war came a shortage of metal, and the industry switched to dry pet food. Dry food captured 85 percent of the market by war's end.

By 1960, 3,000 companies produced 15,000 brands of pet food, with canned foods capturing a 60 percent market share. By 1972 these figures had dropped to 1,500 companies with 10,000 brands, and by 1987 these figures had shrunk even further to 150 companies producing 1,200 brands.

Digests

Small Animal Clinical Nutrition states:

> Digest is probably the most important factor discovered in recent years for enhancing the palatability of dry food for cats and, to a lesser degree, dogs.

In switching from a commercial diet to a home prepared one, be prepared for your pet's addiction to digest. That is why it is so often necessary to make a lengthy dietary transition.

Controlled enzymatic degradation of chicken viscera creates digest. Starting materials other than viscera, such as fish, liver, and cow lungs, require adding a proteolytic enzyme. Degradation of the tissues occurs by adjusting the pH, which inhibits putrefying bacteria while encouraging autolysis (self-digestion). Creating a pH unfavorable for further activity by adding a strong acid (usually phosphoric), stops the process.

Imagine what this huge vat of warm, blended entrails looks and smells like after three weeks!

Dry pet foods receive pasteurized dried digest surface applied at 1–3 percent concentration for dog and 1–7 percent for cat. Different digests justify different flavor designations for essentially the same pet food. With billions of dollars at stake, information about digest is hard to obtain, since the type of enzymes and substrate mixtures used in digest manufacturing are closely guarded trade secrets.

Types of food

A bewildering array of pet foods is available. Top sales goes to dry dog, followed by canned cat, canned dog, dry cat, dog treat, soft-dry dog (such as *Dinner Rounds),* semi-moist cat, semi-moist dog, and cat treat. Most of these contain varying amounts of preservatives such as BHA, preserving food and profits for the retailer. Anitra Frazier vetoes semi-moist foods containing preservatives, which gives a shelf life "approaching infinity." Meat by-products (i.e., waste products), banned in British pet foods since 1990, are prominent in foods sold in this country.

Extruded pet foods

From its origin in the laboratories of Ralston Purina in the 1950s, extruded foods comprise the bulk of pet foods today. A dazzling array of shapes, textures, colors and combinations of these variables is possible through extrusion cooking.

Ingredients are mixed together, forming a slurry, and heated to as much as 200°C. High pressure pushes it through a die where a spinning blade slices off pieces. These ride on hot air past nozzles spraying a coating. Extrusion "gelatinizes" ingredients by breaking down and reforming ingredient molecules, resulting in an expanded, fused, porous and durable structure.

Major league

Dominant players dividing a multibillion dollar jackpot were: Ralson Purina (24.2 percent), Friskies PetCare (14.9 percent), Kal Kan (12.5 percent), Heinz (11.4 percent), Quaker (9.0 percent) and Alpo (8.6 percent), leaving 19.4 percent for all others.

Ralston Purina

In 1926, Ralston Purina started a kennel to determine palatability in dog food. Their *Dog Chow Checkers* began selling through feed stores in 1927. In 1933, Admiral Richard Byrd fed 50 tons of this product to his sled dogs on his Antartic expedition.

By the mid-1950's, Ralson had developed extruders that added bulk to its cereals and then applied the same process to its dog food. In 1958 it became the largest selling dog food in the United States.

Not to have all of its kibbles in one bag, Ralston Purina with 1991 pet food sales of $1,683,000,000, owns Eveready Battery Company (the ubiquitous Energizer bunny), BeechNut (baby foods) and Continental Baking Company. Their far reaching vision brings us products like *Nintendo Cereal* and *Breakfast with Barbie.*

Carnation

Carnation occupies position number two with 1991 sales of $864,000,000. Their main line is *Friskies* but they also market *Chew-eez, Wagtime Biscuits,* as well as cat litter *(Kleen Kitty Cat Litter)*. A cash cow, Carnation funnels its profits to the huge Nestlé SA, headquartered in Switzerland where it harbors enormous sums of money (1989 income of $30,600,000,000).

Kal Kan

Running in third place for pet food dollars, California's Kal Kan Foods is a unit of Mars, Inc. (Virginia), the world's *largest* producer of pet foods. It may be more familiar as *Pedigree* brand for dogs and *Whiskas* and *Sheba* brands for cats. Kal Kan spent $50,000,000 in 1991 advertising their new *Expert* line.

Heinz

Heinz Pet Products Company, best known for Morris, racked up sales of $750,600,000 in 1991. Brands include *Skippy, Vets, Sturdy, Glamour Puss, Figaro,* and *9-Lives.* A glimmer of light from the right direction comes from their "dolphin safe" pet foods, but what we *really* want is "animal safe!"

Quaker Oats

In Rockford, Illinois, the Chappel Brothers canned horse flesh under the name *Ken-L-Ration*. Public opinion decried this use of horses, however, and Congress made interstate transport difficult. Facing ruin, they turned to dry dog food in the 1930's.

Quaker Oats bought Chappel Brothers in 1942, and their main product line, Gaines, the next year. Both *Ken-L-Ration* and *Puss 'N Boots* became legendary. With 1991 pet food sales of $679,100,000, Quaker promotes new products such as *Frisbee Flying Dog Treats*.

Don't tell

In 1942, Dr. Graham, working for Quaker, published a study on four sets of rats. The first ate whole wheat, water, vitamins and minerals. The second set received Quaker *Puffed Wheat* along with the same nutrients. A third set received water and chemical nutrients, and the fourth set consumed just water and white sugar. The first set lived over a year on the diet, the second set lived about eight weeks. The animals on a white sugar and water diet lasted a month. But the shocker, the fourth set, lived just two weeks! This wasn't malnutrition. Something toxic killed the rats and it came from the *Puffed Wheat*.

Proteins are very similar to certain toxins in molecular structure, and the puffing process puts grains under 1500 pounds per square inch pressure. Numerous chemical changes take place when grains are released at that pressure, some of which turn a nutritious grain poisonous. When reminded about the 1942 study, the past president of Quaker, Robert D. Stuart III, said, "I know people should throw it on brides and grooms at weddings, but if they insist on sticking it in their mouths, can I help it? Besides, we made $9,000,000 on the stuff last year."

Quaker doesn't do animal feeding studies on their "people" food anymore. These tests may show their tampered foods are incapable of sustaining life. But they spend lavishly in testing pet foods. For more insider news about Quaker, read *Fighting the Food Giants,* by Paul A. Stitt.

Hill's Science Diet

Hill's Pet Products, in this country's heartland (Kansas), manufactures the specialty leader, Science Diet, sold only through pet professionals to the tune of $550,000,000. They jealously guard the name "science," as their private property, recently suing Kal Kan for printing "A Scientific Diet" on its *Expert* line. They also sued Ralston Purina for *intending* to use "Science Select" on a forthcoming product.

Pet owners often believe they are using the finest food possible by using Science Diet. The company stresses their product's popularity with veterinarians. But most veterinarians are not experts on nutrition. Much of their information comes from pet food manufacturers trying to sell their products.

Science Diet states emphatically "only the highest quality ingredients are used." Their *Feline Maintenance* lists poultry by-product meal as its dominant ingredient. This is the stuff that was thrown away until slaughterhouses found that pet food manufacturers, looking for cheaper ingredients, would *pay* for it. Veterinarian Alfred Plechner defines by-products as "diseased tissue, pus, hair [feathers], assorted slaughterhouse rejects, and carcasses in varying stages of decomposition.

Their advertising states, "When you select Science Diet brand products for your cat or dog, you're choosing much more than just pet food." But do we really want the *much more,* such as the suspected carcinogen, BHA (butylated hydroxyanisole), contained in their formulations? This controversial preservative is accused of causing liver damage, behavior problems, and brain defects. A 1980 report to the FDA reported that it causes a 50% decreased activity in brain cholinesterase, and could affect the normal sequence of neurological development in young animals. Unfortunately for growing pets, Science Diet includes this in their puppy and kitten formulations as well. BHA is commonly used in other manufacturers' preparations as well. It may not even *do* what it's reputedly useful for, since Eastman Chemical Products stated in one of its publications, "BHA and/or BHT are not found to provide significant improvement in the stability of vegetable oils."

Other ingredients include poultry digest (for palatability) and the preservative propyl gallate, a suspected carcinogen associated with liver damage and birth defects.

Science Diet claims, "we do everything we can to make our food as healthy as possible," but in their search for longer shelf life (presumably for veterinarians who only order occasionally) they add Monsanto's potent chemical preservative, ethoxyquin. In this country, suspiciously, the only foods it's allowed in for human consumption are paprika and chili powder. Reference manuals list it not only as a feed preservative, but also as a fungicide, herbicide, insecticide, and rubber stabilizer. There have been no long term studies of ethoxyquin with dogs or cats, but breeders relate that problems with skin and missed breeding disappear when ethoxyquin preserved foods are removed from the diet. Many reputable companies steer clear of ethoxyquin.

A better way of preserving fats is by using vitamins E and C. In a paper presented by the Department of Vitamin and Nutritional Research of Hoffman-La Roche & Co., Dr. H. Klaui stated: "In addition to the advantage of being toxicologically well examined and being natural ingredients of food …these compounds possess nutritive value as vitamins or provitamins."

Hill's Pet Products is the fast growing subsidiary and *golden egg* of Colgate-Palmolive (the giant personal care and household cleaning company). If Science Diet used healthier ingredients, increased costs could put a crack in that egg.

Alpo Petfoods, Inc.

Located in Pennsylvania with pet food sales of $482,900,000, Alpo is a subsidiary of Grand Metropolitan, PLC, with sales of over $15 billion. Other stable mates include Pillsbury, Burger King, Carillon Importers, and Heublein.

Doane Products Company

Missouri's Doane Products Company is the second largest manufacturer of dry pet food in the United States with 1991 sales of $400,000,000. Most of its products are private labeled for giants such as Wal-Mart.

Iams Company

In the 1950s, Paul Iams developed the first meat based dry dog food, *Iams 999.* The Iams Company, located in Ohio, sells its products through pet professionals. Sales of their two brands, Iams and Eukanuba, raked in $220,000,000 in 1991.

Nabisco Brands, Inc.

When Jack Spratt came to America in 1895, he had no competition until the Bennet Biscuit Company produced *Milk Bone* Dog and Puppy Foods. Although put into boxes, they often turned rancid without preservatives.

Nabisco Brands, Inc. headquartered in New Jersey, bought *Milk-Bone* in 1931. When they took on the line, their 3,000 salesmen convinced grocers to stock *Milk-Bone*. At the time this was an incredible breakthrough, since it was understood that dog foods, made from waste products, had no business sitting next to human foods.

A recent introduction is *Milk-Bone Tarter Control* biscuits. Nabisco merged with R.J. Reynolds (tobacco) in 1985, bought by Kohlberg Kravis Roberts in 1988. At this writing, Nabisco apparently wants out of the bone business, but so far no bites.

Nature's Recipe

Many purchasers of *Vegedog* formerly used Nature's Recipe formulations. Originally made in response to those who demanded a non-meat food for their dogs due to allergic reactions, Nature's Recipe *Non-Meat Kibble* dog food, advertised as "nutritionally complete," may lead to serious problems for puppies.

Richard Browning told us that after his puppy, Intrepid X, suffered a painful injury, he took him to a local veterinarian for treatment. When three weeks passed with no improvement, Rick took Treppy to the vet again, who now advised an orthopedic specialist. The new vet took X-rays and found an abnormal *spongy* texture to Treppy's bones, apparently caused by a prolonged dietary deficiency of body building minerals. By this time Richard's vet bills amounted to over $200.

Since Treppy was raised on Nature's Recipe *Non-Meat Kibble*, Rick called the company in California. He told them of the X-rays, pointing out that their kibble stated, "A Complete and Balanced Diet." At that point the company spokesman interrupted, "This formulation is *not* meant for growth."

Rick, although not liking the idea of supporting a company killing sheep for dogs, fed Nature's Recipe because "like many things that can lead one wrong, it was easy." He faxed us, "There is absolutely no mention on the packaging or literature that it is not recommended for puppies, which borders on criminal."

His suffering dog proved that one formulation cannot meet all stages in a dog's life. We sent *Vegedog* containing two charts, one for portion sizes, and the other for supplement concentration gauged to stages in a dog's life. Treppy is now doing fine.

Slaughterhouse products

In talking with the owner (a non-vegetarian) of Nature's Recipe a few years ago, he stated that dogs and cats are better off eating meat. He formulates non-meat recipes only because of their hypo-allergenic properties. Dogs hypersensitive to meat antigens have the most trouble with the flesh of cows, followed by that from horses, pigs, fish, chickens, and sheep.

Vitamin D3 found in Nature's Recipe formulations comes from lanolin extracted from wool of (usually slaughtered) sheep. Most of their products contain slaughtered animal parts (like the rest of the sheep). Apparently they don't consider it a conflict of interest to sell vegetarian foods out one door as slaughtered deer come in the next, since their latest offering is *Venison and Rice.*

Caveat emptor

The federal government doesn't permit selling decomposed fish for human consumption. That's why millions of cans of tuna, from a plant since closed down by the Canadian government due to unsanitary conditions, originally sold as *7th Heaven* cat food. Entrepreneurs, sensing an opportunity for profit, changed the labels on thousands of cans.

Some of the 25 to 50 million cans of tuna, packaged in 1985 by the Canadian cannery, showed up in supermarkets in 1992 as "Ocean King Chunk Light Tuna in Water." An FDA spokesman, commenting on the federal seizure of some 38,640 cans, stated,

"But who wants to eat decomposed cat food?" Who wants to *feed* decomposed food? Don't look *too* close at what's in that can.

Are they complete?

Just coming on the market are vegetarian cat foods. Some, advertised as complete and meeting NRC requirements, unfortunately are more fancy than fact. For instance, *Evolution K9,* recently introduced, leaves one suspicious with their presentation and careless attention to detail.

It claims to supply "four times the national research council's [sic] requirements for all vitamins and trace minerals," which (if true) would create dangerous imbalances.

If that isn't enough, it advertises "no ash." Seriously, are we to believe that it supplies 400% of the mineral requirements with no ash? *Every* other food processor calls minerals *ash.*

Another point that has far reaching health ramifications is Evolution's total lack of arachidonate, in spite of stating that it meets all NRC requirements, which include this fatty acid.

It states that "there are no animal products in Evolution," but it includes vitamin D3 (from sheep), and powdered cheese as ingredients. Even soy based cheeses usually contain casein, a milk protein.

Another company, Wysong also introduced a vegetarian cat food: Canine/Feline Anergen III, advertised as meeting all NRC recommendations except for protein (it is too low). On closer examination, it too fails to provide a source for arachidonic acid.

The future

Many people ask HOANA for a prepared vegetarian pet food. We have not had the necessary financial resources to bring this project to fruition, but stay tuned in...

Appendix 2

TECHNICAL DETAILS

Pet food manufacturers will soon have a new set of requirements by The Association of American Feed Control Officials (AAFCO), which historically has used the National Research Council as its "recognized authority" on animal nutrition.

NRC in 1985 and 1986 revised their publications on cat and (respectively) dog requirements, using "purified" ingredients, leaving it up to processors to determine bioavailability. New requirements by AAFCO's Canine Nutrition Expert Subcommittee and the Feline Nutrition Expert Subcommittee are based upon commonly-used ingredients, making them of more practical use.

Presently using NRC requirements as updated by research, we'll switch to new AAFCO guidelines when available in 1993.

Carnitine and cardiomyopathy

In 1988, some scientists speculated that DCM in dogs may be related to a deficiency of carnitine, a water soluble amino acid like substance found in animal tissues. Paul Pion, who first discovered the taurine/cardiomyopathy link for cats, recently stated, "The evidence is not at all strong enough to prove a cause/effect relationship. Most dogs that we treat for dilated cardiomyopathy (DCM) with carnitine have NOT responded. It is expensive to treat with carnitine — there is NO reason why owners should go running out to buy caritine at this time."

AAFCO's Canine Nutrition Expert Subcommittee does not consider it a dietary requirement in their new recommendations.

About the analyses

Bioavailability is factored in for dietary ingredients. "Contains" reflects net (not crude) amounts. Canola oil was used.

CAT MAINTENANCE

(Based upon a 10-pound cat using garbanzo bean recipe #1)

WATER CONTENT   49.3%

Nutrient (mg)	Requirement	Contains	% DW
Ash			5.6
Carbohydrate			31.5
Fat			30.7
Fiber			2.8
Protein (g)	10.2	16.1	20.1
Calories	362.9	365.4	
Calcium	584.6	638.7	.80
Copper	.37	.50	.0007
Iodine	.03	.99	.0012
Iron	5.8	13.6	.017
Magnesium	29.2	86.9	.11
Manganese	.37	.63	.0008
Phosphorus	438	499	.62
Potassium	292	659	.82
Selenium	.0073	.0074	.000009
Sodium	36	42	.05
Zinc	3.6	4.2	.0053
Biotin	.005	.018	.000002
Choline	175	202	.25
Folic Acid	.06	.40	.0004
Niacin	2.9	18.5	.02
Pantothenic	.36	1.62	.002
Vit A retinol (IU)	243	257	
Vit B1 Thiamin	.37	11.0	.01
Vit B2 Riboflavin	.29	3.66	.005
Vit B6 Pyridoxine	.29	.59	.00074
Vit B12	.0015	.0015	.000002
Vit C	N/A	24.8	.031

Nutrient (mg)	Requirement	Contains	% DW
Vit D (IU)	36.5	38.7	
Vit E (IU)	2.2	10.3	
Alanine	N/A	1067	1.33
Arginine	731	967	1.21
Aspartic Acid	N/A	1896	2.37
Cystine	N/A	229	.29
Glutamic Acid	N/A	3043	3.81
Glycine	N/A	767	.96
Histidine	219	501	.63
Isoleucine	365	759	.95
Leucine	877	1274	1.59
Lysine	585	1241	1.55
Methionine	292	292	.36
" plus Cystine	548	548	.68
Phenylalanine	292	813	1.02
" plus Tyrosine	621	1080	1.35
Proline	N/A	749	.94
Serine	N/A	810	1.01
Taurine	58.5	61.9	.08
Threonine	511	743	.93
Tryptophan	110	188	.24
Tyrosine	N/A	266	.33
Valine	438	942	1.18
Linoleic Acid	365	1928	2.41
Linolenic Acid	N/A	213	.27
Arachidonate (see note)	15.6	8.0	.010

A note about arachidonate

According to research by Marnie MacDonald and others, published in *American Journal of Veterinary Research,* reproduction (the severest test of arachidonate deficiency), is normal for cats fed one-fourth (3.9mg) of the arachidonate requirement (15.6mg) *if* animal fat 22:6n3 (found in tuna oil) is absent.

For kittens and queens, HOANA meets the full requirement, giving a 400-percent safety factor to cats not fed tuna.

CAT GROWTH

{Based upon a 2.2-pound kitten using garbanzo bean recipe #1}
WATER CONTENT   50.1%

Nutrient (mg)	Requirement	Contains	% DW
Ash			6.3
Carbohydrate			33.5
Fat			26.5
Fiber			2.9
Protein (g)	12.5	12.9	21.3
Calories	250.0	260.1	
Calcium	416.2	453.2	.75
Copper	.26	.41	.0007
Iodine	.02	.1.4	.0023
Iron	4.2	10.1	.017
Magnesium	20.8	75.4	.13
Manganese	.26	.50	.0009
Phosphorus	312	375	.62
Potassium	208	548	.91
Selenium	.0052	.0053	.000009
Sodium	26	56	.09
Zinc	2.6	3.4	.0057
Biotin	.004	.014	.000002
Choline	125	175	.29
Folic Acid	.04	.29	.0005
Niacin	2.1	15.0	.025
Pantothenic	.26	1.30	.002
Vit A retinol (IU)	312	334	
Vit B1 Thiamin	.26	8.89	.015
Vit B2 Riboflavin	.21	3.0	.005
Vit B6 Pyridoxine	.21	.48	.00079
Vit B12	.0010	.0011	.000002
Vit C	N/A	22.7	.038
Vit D (IU)	26.0	27.9	
Vit E (IU)	1.6	8.6	
Alanine	N/A	860	1.43
Arginine	520	771	1.28

Nutrient (mg)	Requirement	Contains	% DW
Aspartic Acid	N/A	1514	2.51
Cystine	N/A	187	.31
Glutamic Acid	N/A	2434	4.04
Glycine	N/A	617	1.02
Histidine	156	400	.66
Isoleucine	260	609	1.01
Leucine	624	1018	1.69
Lysine	416	993	1.65
Methionine	208	228	.38
" plus Cystine	390	390	.64
Phenylalanine	208	647	1.08
" plus Tyrosine	442	857	1.42
Proline	N/A	600	1.00
Serine	N/A	650	1.08
Taurine	42	45	.08
Threonine	364	596	.99
Tryptophan	78	152	.25
Tyrosine	N/A	210	.35
Valine	312	755	1.25
Linoleic Acid	260	1247	2.07
Linolenic Acid	N/A	148	.25
Arachidonate	11.1	11.4	.019

DOG MAINTENANCE

NRC prints two columns of figures for canine requirements, one for growth and one for maintenance. For protein, a note is appended, "Quantities [protein] sufficient to supply the minimum amounts of available indispensable and dispensable amino acids as specified below." We meet protein requirements by meeting individual amino acid requirements. The closer the supply of the complement of amino acids to the requirement, the lower the percentage of protein required in the dog's diet.

(For a 44-pound adult dog using garbanzo bean recipe #1)

WATER CONTENT   65.9%

Nutrient (mg)	Requirement	Contains	% DW
Ash			4.7
Carbohydrate			47.2
Fat			11.9
Fiber			5.1
Protein (g)		68.6	18.9
Calories	1183	1194	
Calcium	2380	2574	.71
Copper	1.2	2.3	.0006
Iodine	.2	.25	.0001
Iron	13	93	.026
Magnesium	164	449	.12
Manganese	2.0	3.9	.0011
Phosphorus	1780	2104	.58
Potassium	1780	2517	.69
Selenium	.044	.050	.000014
Sodium	220	220	.06
Zinc	14.4	18.8	.0049
Biotin	N/A	.042	.000012
Choline	500	911	.25
Folic Acid	.08	1.79	.0005
Niacin	4.5	17.5	.005
Pantothenic	4.0	5.0	.0014
Vit A activity (IU)	1500	1651	
Vit B1 Thiamin	.4	9.7	.003
Vit B2 Riboflavin	1.0	3.1	.0009
Vit B6 Pyridoxine	.4	1.2	.00033
Vit B12	.01	.01	.000003
Vit C	N/A	15.7	.004
Vit D (IU)	160	170	
Vit E (IU)	10	29	
Alanine	N/A	3380	.93
Arginine	420	4680	1.28
Aspartic Acid	N/A	8265	2.28
Cystine	N/A	793	.22
Glutamic Acid	N/A	13011	3.59
Glycine	N/A	2914	.80
Histidine	440	2137	.59

Nutrient (mg)	Requirement	Contains	% DW
Isoleucine	960	2871	.79
Leucine	1680	5298	1.46
Lysine	1000	4767	1.31
Methionine	N/A	992	.27
" plus Cystine	600	1785	.49
Phenylalanine	N/A	3918	1.08
" plus Tyrosine	1720	5951	1.64
Proline	N/A	3105	.86
Serine	N/A	3446	.95
Threonine	880	2737	.75
Tryptophan	260	836	.23
Tyrosine	N/A	2033	.56
Valine	1200	3404	.94
Linoleic Acid	4000	13835	3.38
Linolenic Acid	N/A	1273	.35

DOG GROWTH

(For a 6.6-pound pup in early growth using garbanzo bean recipe #1)

WATER CONTENT   66.0%

Nutrient (mg)	Requirement	Contains	% DW
Ash			4.0
Carbohydrate			47.3
Fat			12.0
Fiber			5.1
Protein (g)		43.2	19.1
Calories	737	748.2	
Calcium	960	1221.6	.54
Copper	.5	1.4	.0006
Iodine	.10	.12	.0001
Iron	5.2	57.8	.026
Magnesium	66	281	.12
Manganese	.8	2.4	.0011
Phosphorus	720	1215	.54
Potassium	720	1583	.70
Selenium	.018	.27	.000014
Sodium	90	116	.05

Nutrient (mg)	Requirement	Contains	% DW
Zinc	10.4	5.8	.0046
Biotin	N/A	.027	.000012
Choline	150	545	.24
Folic Acid	.024	1.12	.0005
Niacin	1.4	11.5	.005
Pantothenic	1.2	3.1	.0014
Vit A activity (IU)	1606	778	
Vit B$_1$ Thiamin	.2	6.4	.003
Vit B$_2$ Riboflavin	.3	2.1	.0009
Vit B$_6$ Pyridoxine	.2	.7	.00033
Vit B$_{12}$	.003	.005	.000002
Vit C	N/A	7.8	.0035
Vit D (IU)	66	79	
Vit E (IU)	3.6	8.3	.004
Alanine	N/A	2136	.95
Arginine	822	2922	1.29
Aspartic Acid	N/A	5199	2.30
Cystine	N/A	500	.22
Glutamic Acid	N/A	8185	3.62
Glycine	N/A	1836	.81
Histidine	294	1344	.59
Isoleucine	588	1809	.80
Leucine	954	3334	1.48
Lysine	840	3003	1.33
Methionine	N/A	625	.28
" plus Cystine	636	1125	.50
Phenylalanine	N/A	2462	1.09
" plus Tyrosine	1170	3733	1.65
Proline	N/A	1954	.87
Serine	N/A	2168	.96
Threonine	762	1725	.76
Tryptophan	246	526	.23
Tyrosine	N/A	1272	.56
Valine	630	2147	.95
Linoleic Acid	1620	5963	2.64
Linolenic Acid	N/A	3051	1.35

Appendix 3

RESOURCES

American Holistic Veterinary Medical Association
2214 Old Emmorton Road
Bel Air MD 21015
Phone (410) 569-0795
Send SASE for list of local holistic vets in your area

Biotec Foods-Biovet International
3638 Waialae Avenue
Honolulu, HI 66816
Phone (800) 468-7578
S.O.D. — catalase supplements

Homeopathic Educational Services
2124 Kittredge St.
Berkeley, CA 94704.

International Veterinary Acupuncture Society
Meredith Snader, VMD, Exec. Director
Chester Springs, PA 19425
Phone (215) 827-7742

Katz Go Vegan
Box 161
The Vegan Society
7 Battle Road
Saint Leonards on the Sea
East Sussex TN377AA
England
Phone 0424 441868

Microlight Nutritional Products
124 Rhodesia Beach Rd.
Bay Center, WA 98527
Phone (800) 338-2821
Spirulina

National Center for Homeopathy
1500 Massachusetts Ave. NW
Suite 42
Washington DC 20005

National Enzyme Company
P. O. Box 128 - Hwy. 160
Forsyth, MO 65653
Phone (417) 546-4796

Peaceable Kingdom
P. O. Box 8756
Greenville SC 29604
"Peaceable Alternatives"

**People for the Ethical
Treatment of Animals
(PETA)**
P. O. Box 96684
Washington DC 20077-7538

TGV - Vegan Products
Postbus 377,
6800 AJ Arnhem
The Netherlands
Phone (0) 85-420746

Universal Foods Corporation
433 East Michigan Street
Milwaukee, WS53201
Phone (414) 271-6755
Nutritional yeast

Vegans In South Africa
Box 36242
Glosderry 7702
South Africa

Wow-Bow Distributors
309 Burr Road
Northport, NY 11731
(516) 499-8572
Vegetarian pet biscuits

Below is an excerpt from "Outermost House" that expresses the philosophies of Peaceable Kingdom.

> We need another and a wiser and perhaps a more mystical concept of animals. Remote from universal nature, and living by complicated artifice, man in civilization surveys the creatures through the glass of his knowledge and sees thereby a feather magnified and the whole image in distortion. We patronize them for their incompleteness, for their tragic fate of having taken form so far below ourselves. And therein we err, and greatly err. For the animal shall not be measured by man.
>
> In a world older and more complete than ours they move finished and complete, gifted with extensions of the senses we have lost or never attained, living by voices we shall never hear.
>
> They are not brethren; they are not underlings; they are other nations, caught with ourselves in the net of life and time, fellow prisoners of the splendor and travail of the earth.
>
> Henry Beston

BIBLIOGRAPHY

"Acetone." *Encylopaedia Britannica.* 15th ed. 1976.

Adams, C.F. Nutritive Value of American Foods. USDA Handbook No. 456, Washington: GPO, 1975.

Aguirre, G. "Retinal degeneration associated with the feeding of dog foods to cats." *J. Am. Vet. Med. Assoc.* 172 (1978): 791-96.

Aihara, H. *Acid and Alkaline.* 5th ed. Oroville: George Ohsawa Macrobiotic Foundation, 1986.

Alderton, D. *The Dog Care Manual.* London: Quarto Pub. Ltd., 1986.

Anderson, P., et al. "Nitrogen Requirement of the kitten." *Am. J. Vet. Res.* 41 (1980): 1646-49.

"A Rat May Be Somebody's Mother." *Vegetarian Times* May 1992: 24-25.

Authur, G., Noakes, D., & Pearson, H. *Vet. Reproduction & Obstetrics.* 5th ed. London: Bailliere Tindall, 1982.

Axelson, M., et. al. "Soya — a dietary source of the non-steroidal oestrogen equol in man and animals." *J. Endocr.* 102 (1984): 49-56.

Balch, J.F. & Balch, P. *Prescription for Nutritional Healing.* Garden City Park: Avery Pub. Group Inc., 1990.

Beadle, M. *The Cat.* New York: Simon & Schuster, Inc.,1977.

Belfield, W. & Zucker, M. *The Very Healthy Cat Book.* New York: McGraw-Hill Book Co., 1983.

— , & — . *How to Have a Healthier Dog.* New York: Doubleday & Co., 1981.

Berson, E., & Hayes, K. "Retinal degeneration in cats fed casein. I. Taurine deficiency." *Invest. Ophthalmol.* 15 (1976): 47-52.

— , et al. "Retinal degeneration in cats fed casein. II. Supplementation with methionine, cysteine, or taurine. *Invest. Ophthalmol.* 15 (1976): 52-61.

Bible, The. Trans. (1611), King James. Philadelphia: A.J. Holman Co.

Black, D. "Excretory System Diseases. *Encyclopaedia Britannica.* 15th ed. 1976.

Block, J. et al. *Amino Acid Handbook.* Springfield: Charles C. Thomas, 1956.

Booth, N. & McDonald, L. *Vet. Pharmacology and Therapeutics.* 5th ed. Ames: The Iowa State Univ. Press, 1982.

Bryant, D. *Pet Cats.* New York: Ives Washburn, Inc., 1963.

Bueler, L. *Wild Dogs of the World.* New York: Stein and Day, 1980.

Burger, I. & Barnett, K. "The taurine requirement of the adult cat. *J. Small Ani. Practi.* 23 (1982): 533-37.

Bush, B. *The Cat Care Question and Answer Book.* London: Macdonald & Co. (Publishers) Ltd., 1981.

Chatterjee, I.B. "Evolution and the Biosynthesis of Ascorbic Acid." *Science* 21 Dec 1973: 1271.

Cheraskin, E., Ringsdorf, W. Jr., & Sisley, E. *The Vitamin C Connection.* New York: Harper & Row, 1983.

Cohn, J. "Surprising cheetah genetics." *BioScience.* 36 (1986): 358-62.

Collins, D. *The Collins Guide to Dog Nutrition.* 2nd ed. New York: Howell Book House, Inc., 1987.

Cone, J., Coine, A., & George, R. *Feeding Fido.* McLean: EPM Pub., Inc., 1982.

Conley, C.L. "Blood, Human." *Encylopaedia Britannica.* 15th ed. 1976.

Costa, P., & Hoskins, J. "The Role of Taurine in Cats." *Compendium on Continuing Education for the Practicing Veterinarian.* Sep 1990.

Davidson, M.K., and Mahan, L.K. *Food, Nutrition and Diet Therapy.* Philadelphia: W.B. Saunders Co., 1979.

Deady, J. et al. "Effects of level of dietary glutamic acid and thiamin on food intake, weight gain, plasma amino acids, and thiamin status of growing kittens. *J. Nutri.* 111 (1981): 1568-79.

Diehl, K. "The Natural Animal." *Body Mind Spirit.* Sep/Oct. 1992: 40-45.

"Diet and disease." *Pet Food Industry* Mar/Apr. 1992: 28.

"Dog food history." *Pet Food Industry* Sep/Oct. 1989: 40.

Donadio, Ola. *Repel Fleas Nutritionally.* Fort Lauderdale: The Pet Health Publications, 1979.

Eckhouse, J. "How Dogs and Cats Get Recycled Into Pet Food." *San Francisco Chronicle:* 19 Feb 1990.

Edwards, D. "Feeding a Finicky Cat." *Cat Fancy.* Jan. 1992: 17-19.

Ehret, A. *Mucusless Diet Healing System.* 15th ed. Beaumont: Ehret Literature Pub. Co., 1972.

Ewer, R. *The Carnivores.* Ithaca: Cornell Univ. Press, 1973.

Fireman, J. ed. *Cat Catalog.* New York: Greenwich House, 1982.

Fox, M *Understanding Your Cat.* New York: Bantam Books, Inc., 1977.

— . *Agricide.* New York: Schocken Books, 1986.

Frankel, T. Manuscript of *Essential fatty acid deficiency in the cat.* Ph.D. thesis. Wollfson Coll., Univ. Cambridge, U.K.., 1980.

Frazier, A., & Eckroate, N. *The Natural Cat.* San Francisco: Harbor Pub., 1981.

— , & — . *It's A Cat's Life.* New York: Berkley Books, 1990.

—, & —. *The New Natural Cat*. New York: Dutton, 1990.

Gaines Dog Research Center. *Basic Guide to Canine Nutrition*. 3rd ed. White Plains: General Foods Corp., 1974.

Galli, C. et al. "Comparative effects of olive oil and other edible fats on brain structural lipids during development." *Lipids, Vol. 1: Biochemistry*. New York: Raven Press, 1976.

Gosselin, S., et al. "Veno-occlusive Disease of the Liver in Captive Cheetah." *Vet. Pathol.* 25 (1988) 48-57.

Graf, E. & Eaton, J. "Effects of phytate on mineral bioavailability in mice." *J. Nutri.* 114 (1984): 1192-98.

Gershoff, S., Legg, M., & Hegsted, D. "Adaptation to different calcium intakes in dogs. *J. Nutr.* 64 (1957): 303-12.

Gosselin, S., et. al. "Veno-occlusive Disease of the Liver in Captive Cheetah." *Vet. Pathol.* 25 (1987): 48-57.

Gregory, D. *Dick Gregory's Natural Diet for Folks Who Eat: Cookin' with Mother Nature*. New York: Harper & Row, 1973.

Guthrie, H.A., *Introductory Nutrition*. St. Louis: The C.V. Mosby Co., 1975.

Guyton, A. *Basic Human Physiology*. Philadelphia: W. B. Saunders Co., 1977.

—. *Function of the Human Body*. Philadelphia: W. B. Saunders Co., 1964.

Hamilton, R. "'Best medicine' may have adverse effects." *Petfood Industry*. Jul/Aug 1987: 26-27.

Harper, J. *Feed the Kitty-Naturally*. Richland Center: Pet Press, 1991.

— *The Healthy Cat and Dog Cook Book*. Richland Center: Pet Press, 1992.

Hayes, K., Carey, R., & Schmidt, S. "Retinal degeneration associated with taurine deficiency in the cat." *Science*. 188 (1975): 949-50.

Haytowitz, D., & Matthews, R. ed. *Composition of Foods*. USDA Handbook No. 8. Washington: GPO, 1984.

Hedhammer, A., et al. "Overnutrition and skeletal disease." *Cornell Vet.* 64 (1974): 5-135.

Hegsted, M., et al, eds. *Present Knowledge In Nutrition*. New York: The Nutrition Foundation, Inc., 1976.

Heritage, F. *Composition and Facts About Foods*. Mokelumne Hill: Health Research, 1968.

Hesser, J. "Uses and Functionality of Wheat Gluten." In *Gluten Proteins*. Eds. R. Lásztity & F. Békés. Singapore: World Scien. Pub. Co. Pte. Ltd., 1987, 441-55.

Hoff-Jorgensen, E. "The influence of phytic acid on the absorption of calcium and phosphorus. *Biochem.* 40 (1946): 189-92.

Howell, E. *Enzyme Nutrition*. Wayne: Avery Pub. Group Inc., 1985.

— . *Food Enzymes For Health and Longevity*. 1946; rpt. Woodstock Valley: Amangod Press, 1980.

Howard, J. "Carnivora." *Encylopaedia Britannica*. 15th ed. 1976.

Hur, R "Six Inches from Starvation; How and Why America's Topsoil is Disappearing." *Vegetarian Times*, Mar1985: 45-47.

Huxtable, R., & Pasantes-Morales, H., ed. *Taurine in Nutrition and Neurology*. New York: Plenum Press, 1982.

"Industry News." *Pet Food Industry* Jul/Aug. 1987: 10.

" — " *Pet Food Industry* May/Jun. 1991: 18.

Jacobsen, J., & Smith, Jr., L. "Biochemistry and physiology of taurine and taurine derivatives." *Physio. Rev.* 48 (1968): 424-511.

Jacoboson, M. *Eater's Digest*. Garden City: Anchor Books, 1972.

Jaggar, D. "Veterinary Acupuncture." *Vegepet Gazette* Spr1989.

Jenkins, K., & Phillips, P. "The mineral requirements of the dog (the relation of calcium, phosphorus and fat levels to minimal calcium and phosphorus requirements)." *J. Nutr.* 70 (1960): 241-46.

Johnson, P. *Cat Love*. Pownal: Storey Communications, Inc., 1990.

Kaeberle, M. "Vaccine quest." *Pet Veterinarian*. Jul/Aug. 1992: 16-19.

Kallfelz, F "The 'natural' myth." *Petfood Industry*, Sep/Oct 1990: 29-31.

Kane, E., et al. "Zinc deficiency in the cat." *J. Nutr.* 111, (1981): 488-95.

Kay, W., et al. *Euthanasia of the Companion Animal*. Philadelphia: The Charles Press, 1988.

"Killer Cats?" *Pet Veterinarian* Jul/Aug. 1992: 22-23.

Konlande, J. and Robson, J. *Foods & Nutrition Encyclopedia*. 2 vols. Clovis: Pegus Press, 1983.

Kulvinskas, V. *Nutritional Evaluation of Sprouts and Grasses*. Wethersfield: Amango D'Press, 1978.

Landers, A. "Dental care can save pet's life." *The Spokesman-Review:* 30 Mar 92.

Lands, W. ed. *Biochemistry of Arachidonic Acid Metabolism*. Boston: Martinus Nijhoff Pub., 1985.

Lásztity, R. and Békés, F., eds. *Gluten Proteins*. Singapore: World Scientific Pub. Co. Pte. Ltd., 1987.

Lazar, V. "Now a 'Member of the Family.'" *Petfood Industry*. Sep/Oct 1987: 6-7.

Lazarus, P. *Keep Your Pet Healthy The Natural Way*. Indianapolis: The Bobbs-Merrill Co., Inc., 1983.

Lemmon, M. "Arthritis Help." *Vegepet Gazette* Spr/Sum 1991.

— . "Homeopathy." *Vegepet Gazette* Sum 1990.

Levy, J. *The Complete Herbal Handbook for the Dog and Cat.* New York: Arco, 1986.

Lewis, L., Morris, M., & Hand, M. *Small Animal Clinical Nutrition III.* Topeka: Mark Morris Assoc., 1987.

Lloyd, H. *The Red Fox.* London: B.T. Batsford, Ltd., 1980.

Loucks, M. "Ethoxyquin safety disputed." Letters. *Pet Veterinarian* Mar-Apr 1990: 14-15.

MacDonald, M., Rogers, Q., & Morris, J. "Effects of dietary arachidonate deficiency on the aggregation of cat platelets." *Comp. Biochem. Physiol.* 78C (1984): 123-26.

— , — , — . "Nutrition of the domestic cat, a mammalian carnivore." *Annual Review of Nutrition.* 4 (1984): 521-62.

— , — , — . "Role of linoleate as an essential fatty acid for the cat independent of arachidonate synthesis. *J. Nutr.* 113 (1983): 1422-33.

— , et al. "Effects of linoleate and arachidonate deficiencies on reproduction and spermatogenesis in the cat." *J. Nutr.* 114 (1984): 719-28.

— , et al. "Essential fatty acid requirements of cats: pathology of essential fatty acid deficiency." *Am. J. Vet. Res.* 45 (1984): 1310-17.

MacEwen, G. "Fat cats and dogs." *Petfood Industry* Jul/Aug 1989: 30+.

Macfarlane, R.G. "Bleeding and Blood Clotting." *Encylopaedia Britannica.* 15th ed. 1976.

Machlin, L., ed. *Handbook of Vitamins.* New York: Marcel Dekker, Inc., 1984.

Mason, J., & Singer, P. *Animal Factories.* New York: Crown Pub., 1980.

Matta, Michael S., and Wilbraham, Antony C. *Atoms Molecules and Life.* Menlo Park: The Benjamin/Cummings Pub. Co., Inc., 1981.

McGee, H. *On Food and Cooking.* New York: Charles Scribner's Sons, 1984.

McGinnis, T. *Dog & Cat Good Food Book.* Brisbane: Taylor & Ng, 1977.

— . *The Well Cat Book.* New York: Random House Inc., 1975.

Merchant, I.A. & Packer, R.A. *Vet. Bacteriology and Virology.* 5th ed. Ames: The Iowa State College Press: 1956.

Mitchell, H.S., et al. *Nutrition In Health and Disease.* New York: J. B. Lippincott Co., 1968.

Morgan, A., et al. "The effect of acid, neutral, and basic diets on the calcium and phosphorus metabolism of dogs." *Univ. Calif. Pub. Physiol.* 8:61 (1934): 61-106.

Morris, J., & Rogers, Q. "Metabolic basis for some of the nutritional peculiarities of the cat." *J. Small Ani. Pract.* 23 (1982): 599-613.

Murphy, P. "Phytoestrogen Content of Processed Soybean Products." *Food Tech.* Jan (1982): 60-64.

National Research Council. *Nutrient Requirements of Cats.* Washington: National Academy of Sciences, 1978, 1986.

— . *Nutrient Requirements of Dogs.* Washington: National Academy of Sciences, 1985.

— . *Recommended Dietary Allowances.* Washington: National Academy of Sciences, 1974.

Neff, J. "There's a reason this tuna tastes like cat food." *The Spokesman-Review:* 24 Mar 92.

Nowell, I. *Dog Crisis.* New York: St. Martin's Press, Inc., 1978.

"NRC profile." *Pet Food Industry* Mar/Apr. 1992: 10.

O'Brien, S., et. al. "Genetic Basis for Species Vulnerability in the Cheetah." *Science* 227 (1985): 1428-34.

Oliver, M. *Add A Few Sprouts.* New Canaan: Keats Pub., Inc., 1975.

Orr, M., & Watt, B. *Amino Acid Content of Foods.* USDA Home Economics Research Report No. 4 Washington: GPO, 1957.

"Palatability" *Pet Food Industry* Mar/Apr. 1991: 16.

Papas, A. "Antioxidants." *Petfood Industry* May/Jun. 1991: 8+.

Peden, B. *Dogs & Cats Go Vegetarian.* 3rd ed. Hayden Lake: Harbingers of a New Age, 1988.

Pennington, J., & Church, H. *Food Values.* New York: Harper & Row, 1985.

Pike, R, & Brown, M. *Nutrition: An Integrated Approach.* New York: John Wiley & Sons, Inc., 1967.

Pion, P., et al. "Myocardial failure in cats associated with low plasma taurine: a reversible cardiomyopathy. *Science.* 237 (1987): 764-68.

Pitcairn, R., & Pitcairn, S. *Dr. Pitcairn's Complete Guide to Natural Health for Dogs & Cats.* Emmas: Rodale Press, 1982.

Pottenger, Jr., F., *Pottenger's Cats.* La Mesa: Price-Pottenger Nutrition Foundation, Inc., 1983.

Ratnayake, W., & Ackman, R. "A research report on the fatty acid composition of dried ascophyllum nodosum." Halifax: Can. Inst. Fish. Tech., 1987.

Renner, E. *Milk and Dairy Products in Human Nutrition.* Munich: 1983.

"Research Notes." *Pet Food Industry* Nov/Dec. 1988: 49.

" — — ." *Pet Food Industry* Jul/Aug. 1992: 54.

" — —." *Pet Food Industry* May/Jun. 1991: 34.

Rivers, J. "Essential fatty acids in cats." *J. Small Ani. Pract.* 23 (1982): 563-76.

— , & Frankel, T. "Essential fatty acid deficiency." *Br. Med. Bull.* 37 (1981): 59-64.

Robbins, J. *Diet For A New America.* Walpole: Stillpoint Pub., 1987.

Rogers, Q., & Morris, J. "Do cats really need more protein?" *J. Small Ani. Pract.* 23 (1982): 521-32.

— , & — . "Essentiality of amino acids for the growing kitten. *J. Nutr.* 109 (1979): 718-23.

Setchell, K., et al. "Dietary Estrogens — A Probable Cause of Infertility and Liver Disease in Captive Cheetahs." *Gastroenterology* 93 (1987): 225-33.

— , et al. "Nonsteroidal estrogens of dietary origin: possible roles in hormone-dependent disease." *The Amer. Jour. of Clin. Nutr.,* 40 (1984): 569-78.

Shandler, N., & Shandler, M. *How to Make all the Meat You Eat Out of Wheat.* New York: Rawson, Wade Publishers, Inc., 1980.

Shojai, A. "Keeping Cats Healthy." *Cat Fancy.* Sep 1992: 26+.

Shutt, D. "The effects of plant oestrogens on animal reproduction." *Endeavour* 35 (1976): 110-13.

Siegmund, O., ed. *The Merck Vet. Manual.* 5th ed. Rahway: Merck and Co., 1979.

Sinclair, A. "Essential fatty acid requirements of different species." *Proc. Nutr. Soc. Aust.* 10 (1985): 41-48.

— . "Metabolism of linoleic acid in the cat." *Lipids.* 14 (1979).

— . "Determination of essential fatty acid requirements." *Proc. Nutr. Soc. Aust.* 5 (1980): 44-51.

— , et al. "Essential fatty acid deficiency and evidence for arachidonate synthesis in the cat. *Br. J. Nutr.* 46 (1981): 93-96.

Smalley, K., Rogers, Q., & Morris, J. "Methionine requirement of kittens given amino acid diets containing adequate cystine." *Br. J. Nutr.* 49 (1983): 411-17.

Steinman, D. *Diet For A Poisoned Planet.* New York: Harmony Books, 1990.

Stitt, P. Knickelbine, S. & Knickelbine, M. *Fighting the Food Giants.* 2nd ed. Manitowoc: Natural Press, 1981.

Stone, L. *Vitamin C Against Disease.* New York: Grosset & Dunlap, 1972.

Switzer, L. *Spirulina.* Berkeley: Proteus Corp., 1980.

Taylor, D. *You & Your Cat.* New York: Alfred A. Knope, Inc., 1986.

Thorne, C. "Feeding behaviour in the cat — recent advances." *J. Small Ani. Pract.* 23 (1982): 555-62.

Thrash, A. & Thrash, Jr., C. *Nutrition For Vegetarians*. Seale: Thrash Publications, 1982.

Tinoco, J., et al. "Linolenic acid deficiency." *Lipids* 14 (1979): 166-73.

"Top ten." *Pet Food Industry* Jan/Feb. 1990: 4.

Turner, R. "Effect of prolonged feeding of raw carrots on vitamin A content of liver and kidneys in the dog." *Proc. Soc. Exper. Bio. & Med.* 31 (1934): 866-68.

United States Department of Agriculture. *Composition of Foods: Cereal Grains and Pasta, Agriculture Handbook No. 8-20.* Washington: GPO,1989.

Verdeal, K. & Ryan, D. "Naturally-Occurring Estrogens in Plant Foodstuffs — A Review." *Jour. of Food Prot.,* 42 (1979): 577-83.

Walford, L. *Living Resources of the Sea.* New York: Ronald Press Co., 1958.

Walker, B. "Maternal diet and brain fatty acids in young rats." *Lipids* 2 (1967): 497-500.

Webb & Alrod, eds. *Fundamentals of Dairy Chemistry.* Westport: AZ Pub. Co., 1974.

Westbeau, G. *Little Tyke.* Boise: Pacific Press Pub. Assoc., 1956.

White, N. "How Many Tomatoes Gave Their Lives For That Salad?" Huntington: *Our Sunday Visitor,* 26 Apr 92: 19.

Whitney, L. *The Complete Book of Dog Care.* New York: Doubleday & Co., Inc., 1953.

Yogananda, P. *Autobiography of a Yogi.* 9th ed. Los Angeles: Self-Realization Fellowship, 1968.

Zimmer, R. "More veterinarians practicing dentistry." *The Spokesman-Review and Spokane Chronicle* 21 Jan 92: A5.

"Zoo diet to blame for cheetahs' sterility." *New Scientist* 1 Oct 1987: 31.

Zorn, J. W. *Seaweed and Vitality.* New York: Popular Library, 1974.

INDEX